SAS Programming Guidelines

Interview Questions

You'll Most Likely Be Asked

Job Interview Questions Series

VP **Vibrant Publishers**

www.vibrantpublishers.com

SAS Programming Guidelines Interview Questions
You'll Most Likely Be Asked

© 2012, By Vibrant Publishers, USA. All rights reserved. No part of this publication may be reproduced or distributed in any form or by any means, or stored in a database or retrieval system, without the prior permission of the publisher.

ISBN-10: 1480214744
ISBN-13: 9781480214743

Library of Congress Control Number: 2012920665

This publication is designed to provide accurate and authoritative information in regard to the subject matter covered. The author has made every effort in the preparation of this book to ensure the accuracy of the information. However, information in this book is sold without warranty either expressed or implied. The Author or the Publisher will not be liable for any damages caused or alleged to be caused either directly or indirectly by this book.

Vibrant Publishers books are available at special quantity discount for sales promotions, or for use in corporate training programs. For more information please write to **bulkorders@vibrantpublishers.com**

Please email feedback / corrections (technical, grammatical or spelling) to **spellerrors@vibrantpublishers.com**

To access the complete catalogue of Vibrant Publishers, visit **www.vibrantpublishers.com**

Table of Contents

1. Efficient SAS Programming — 7
2. Memory Usage — 11
3. Data Storage Space — 19
4. Best Practices — 29
5. Sorting Strategies — 45
6. Samples — 67
7. Using Indexes — 75
8. Combining Data Vertically — 81
9. Combining Data Horizontally — 85
10. Lookup Tables — 95
11. Formatting Data — 97
12. Tracking Changes — 105
13. HR Questions — 129
    INDEX — 144

This page is intentionally left blank

SAS Programming Guidelines Interview Questions

Review these typical interview questions and think about how you would answer them. Read the answers listed; you will find best possible answers along with strategies and suggestions.

This page is intentionally left blank

Efficient SAS Programming

1: What resources are used to run a SAS program?
Answer:
The six resources used to run a SAS program are:
   a) **Programmer time:** The amount of time taken by the programmer for writing, testing and maintaining the program
   b) **Real time:** The time elapsed while executing a job
   c) **CPU time:** The amount of time the CPU takes to perform a task. The task can be reading data, writing data, calculations or implementation of a logic
   d) **Memory:** The work area memory space used for holding executable programs, data, etc
   e) **Data storage space:** The disk space for storing the data. This is measured in terms of bytes, kilobytes, gigabytes etc.
   f) **I/O:** The read and write operations performed to movie data from the memory to any output device, and vice versa

2: List the factors that need to be considered while assessing the technical environment.
Answer:
The four factors that need to be considered while assessing a technical environment are:
   a) **Hardware:** Available memory, number of CPU's, number of devices connected, network bandwidth, I/O bandwidth, and capability to upgrade
   b) **Operating environment:** The resource allocation & I/O methods
   c) **System load:** This includes the number of users sharing the system, the network traffic, and the predicted increase in load
   d) **SAS environment:** includes all SAS software products installed, number of CPU's, and memory allocated for SAS programming

3: Explain the functionality of the system option STIMER in the Windows environment.

Answer:
STIMER option in the Windows environment specifies that CPU time and real time statistics are tracked and written to the SAS log throughout the SAS session.
Example: The following line of code turns on the STIMER option
options STIMER;

4: What is the function of the option FULLSTIMER in the Windows operating environment?

Answer:
FULLSTIMER option in the Windows environment specifies that all the available resource usage statistics needs to be tracked and written to SAS log throughout the SAS session.
Example:
options FULLSTIMER;

5: Explain the MEMRPT option.

Answer:
The MEMRPT option in the z/OS environment specifies that the memory usage statistics are tracked and written to SAS log throughout the SAS session. This is not available as a separate option in the Windows operating environment.

6: While benchmarking the programming techniques in SAS, why is it necessary to execute each programming technique in separate sessions?

Answer:
It is always necessary to execute each programming technique in separate SAS sessions while benchmarking them the first time a program is read because the operating system might load the code into the cache and retrieve it from the cache when it is referenced. This takes less time. The resource usage necessary to perform this action is referred to as overhead. Using separate sessions minimize the effect of overhead on resource statistics.

7: While doing benchmark tests, when is it advisable to run the code for each programming technique several times?
Answer:
It is advised to run the code for each programming technique several times while benchmarking tests if the system is executing other jobs at the same time. Running the code several times reduces variations in the resource consumption associated with the task and so the average resource usage is known.

8: How do you turn off the FULLSTIMER option?
Answer:
The FULLSTIMER option can be turned off with the following line of code.
options nofullstimer;

9: What steps can be taken to reduce the programmer time?
Answer:
Programmer Time is the amount of time required for the programmer to determine the specifications, write, submit, test and maintain the program. It is difficult to calculate the exact time, but it can be reduced by the use of well-documented programming practices and reuse of SAS code modules.

Memory Usage

10: What is the sequence of action performed in the background while trying to create a data set from another data set?
Answer:
While creating a data set from another data set the following actions take place in the background
  a) The data gets copied from the input data set to a buffer in memory
  b) From the input buffer an observation at a time is written to PDV (Program Data Vector)
  c) Each observation from PDV is written to output buffer when processing is complete
  d) The contents of output buffer are written to disk when the buffer is full

11: Define page and page size.
Answer:
A page is a unit that indicates the data transfer between a storage device and Page size is the amount of data that can be transferred to one buffer in a single I/O operation.

12: What procedure is used to indicate the page size of a data set?
Answer:
The Contents procedure is used to know the page size associated with a data set.
Example: The following Contents procedure issues a message to SAS log indicating the page size associated with the data set exam.clinic1. This also gives the number of data set pages.

Proc contents data = exam.clinic1;
run;

13: Is it possible to control the page size of an output data set?
Answer:
It is possible to control the page size of an output data set by using BUFSIZE= option, which specifies the page size in bytes

Example: The following program creates a data set exam.clinic1 from the data set exam.clinic2. In the following program the BUFSIZE= option specifies a page size of 30720 bytes.

```
options bufsize=30720;
libname exam 'c:\myprog';
data exam.clinic1
    set exam.clinic2;
run;
```

14: What is the default value of the BUFSIZE= option?
Answer:
The default value of the BUFSIZE= option is 0. If BUFSIZE= option is set to zero SAS uses the optimal page size determined by SAS for that operating environment.

15: Is it necessary to specify the BUFSIZE= option every time a data set is processed?
Answer:
No. The BUFSIZE= option is set at the time of creation of data set, and that value of becomes a permanent attribute of the data set. Once it is specified it is used every time the data set is processed.

16: Explain the significance of BUFNO= option.
Answer:
BUFNO= option can be used to specify the number of buffers that are available for reading or writing a SAS data set. It is possible to control the number of pages of data e loaded into the memory with each I/O transfer using this option.
Example: The following program creates a data set exam.clinic1 from the data set exam.clinic2. In the following program the BUFNO= option is given a value of 4, which specifies that 4 buffers are available.

```
options bufno=4;
libname exam 'c:\myprog';
```

```
data exam.clinic1
    set exam.clinic2;
run;
```

17: How do you set the BUFNO= option to the maximum possible number?
Answer:
BUFNO= option can be set to maximum value by giving the value of max in the BUFNO= option. This sets the number of buffers to maximum possible value in the operating environment which is the largest four byte signed integer which is $((2^{31})-1)$ approximately 2 billion.
Example: The following program creates a data set exam.clinic1 from the data set exam.clinic2.In the following program the BUFNO= option is given a value of 4 which specifies that 4 buffers are available.

```
options bufno=4;
libname exam 'c:\myprog';
data exam.clinic1
    set exam.clinic2;
run;
```

18: Is it necessary to specify the BUFNO= option every time a data set is processed?
Answer:
Yes the buffer number is not a permanent attribute of a data set and is valid only for the current SAS session in which it is set.

19: What are the general guidelines for specifying the buffer size and buffer number in the case of small data sets?
Answer:
The main objective behind specifying the buffer size and buffer number is to reduce the number of I/O operations. In the case of small data sets, care must always be taken to allocate as many buffers as there are pages in the data set. This ensures that the

entire data set can be loaded into the memory using a single I/O operation.

20: How does the BUFSIZE= and BUFNO= impact the following program?
```
data exam.clinic1 (bufsize=12288 bufno=10);
set exam.clinic2;
run;
```
Answer:
The above program reads the data set exam.clinic2 and creates exam.clinic1. The BUFSIZE= option specifies that exam.clinic1 is created with a buffer size of 12288 bytes. The BUFNO= option specifies that 10 pages of data are loaded into memory with each I/O transfer.

21: Explain the SASFILE statement.
Answer:
The SASFILE statement is used to hold a SAS data file in memory so that data is available to all subsequent program steps. This reduces the allocation and freeing of memory for buffers.
Example: In the following program the SASFILE statement opens the data set exam.clinic1, allocates the buffer, and reads the data into the memory so it is available to both the proc print as well as the proc means step. The last SASFILE statement closes the SAS data file and makes the buffers free.

```
sasfile exam.clinic1 load;
proc print data= exam.clinic1
    var slno result;
run;
proc means data= exam.clinic1;
run;
sasfile exam.clinic1 close;
```

22: What happens if the size of the file in the memory increases during the execution of SASFILE statement?

Answer:
During the execution of a SASFILE statement SAS allocates the number of buffers based on the number of pages required for the SAS data file and the index file. Once the data file is held in the memory any update operation can be performed. If the files in the memory increase in size during processing then the number of buffers associated also increases.

23: Mention the guidelines to be followed while using SASFILE statement.
Answer:
The following guidelines are followed while using SASFILE statement:
a) Care must be taken to ensure there is sufficient real memory
b) If there is a data file that does not fit into memory completely, then use the data step with the SASFILE statement to create a subset of the file that fits into memory. This saves CPU time since a part of the file resides in memory. Other parts can be processed quickly

24: How is free buffer allocated by the SASFILE statement?
Answer:
The SASFILE statement opens the data file and allocates enough buffers to hold the data in memory. These buffers can be released only when:
a) SASFILE CLOSE statement is used.
Example: In the following program example the SASFILE statement opens the data set exam.clinic1 then allocates the buffer, reads the data into the memory, and it is available to both the proc print as well as proc means step. The last SASFILE statement closes the SAS data file and frees the buffers.

sasfile exam.clinic1 load;
proc print data= exam.clinic1

        var slno result;
run;
proc means data= exam.clinic1;
run;
sasfile exam.clinic1 close;

b) SAS session ends so it frees the buffers and closes the file.

25: Which operations are not allowed in a file opened with SASFILE statement?
Answer:
There are certain operations that cannot be performed on a file opened with sasfile statement, such as replacing the file and renaming the variables.

26: How do you calculate the total number of bytes occupied by a data file if you know the page size?
Answer:
The total number of bytes that a data file occupies can be calculated by multiplying the page size by the number of pages. Example: If the data file exam.clinic1 has a page size of 8192 and number of pages is 900, then the data file occupies 7372800 bytes (8192* 9423).

This page is intentionally left blank

Data Storage Space

27: What factors are considered by SAS when calculating the data storage space required for a SAS data file?
Answer:
The following factors are considered by SAS when calculating the data storage space required for a SAS data file:
   a) Storage space required by the descriptor portion
   b) Storage space required by the observations
   c) Any storage overhead
   d) Storage space required for associated indexes

28: How do a SAS character variable store data and what is the default length of a character variable?
Answer:
SAS character variables store data as one character per byte. The default length of a character variable is 8 bytes.

29: Which step can be taken to reduce the length of a character variable?
Answer:
A length statement can be used to control the length of character variable.
Example: In the following program example the data set exam.clinic1 is created from the data set exam.clinic2. The variable, name, is assigned a value of 5. So the variable name of the data set exam.clinic1 will have a length of 5.

```
data exam.clinic1;
    length name $ 5;
        set exam.clinic2;
run;
```

30: How does SAS store numeric values and what is the default length of a numeric variable?
Answer:
SAS stores numeric values using double precision floating point representation (form of scientific notation). This helps with storing

numbers of large magnitude and to perform computations that requires precision after the decimal point. The default length of numeric variables is 8 bytes.

31: Explain the significance of PROC COMPARE.
Answer:
PROC COMPARE is used to compare the contents of two SAS data sets. It compares the following:
   a) Data set attributes
   b) Variables
   c) Observations
   d) Variable attributes and values of matching variables

Example: The following PROC COMPARE step compares the two data sets exam.result1 and exam.result2 and prints the result in SAS log:

proc compare base= exam.result1
    compare= exam.result2;
run;

32: What all conditions make a data file an ideal candidate for compression?
Answer:
A data file becomes an ideal candidate for compression if it satisfies one or more of the following conditions:
   a) It is large
   b) It has many missing values
   c) It has many lengthy character values
   d) It has repeated characters or binary zeroes
   e) It has repeated values in the variable which are physically stored next to one another

33: Explain the compression of a data set.
Answer:
A SAS data file by default is uncompressed. It can be compressed

to conserve disk space. A data set can be compressed by using the compress= option.
Example: The following program creates a compressed data set exam.result1 from the data set exam.result2. When the data set is created SAS writes a note to the log indicating the percentage of reduction in size obtained by compressing the data set. Here it uses the RLE (Run Length Encoding) Algorithm for compressing the data set. RLE algorithm compresses the observations by reducing the repeated consecutive characters to 2 byte or 3 byte representations.

```
data exam.result1 (compress= YES);
    set exam.result2;
run;
```

34: Which option is used for accessing an observation directly in an uncompressed data set?
Answer:
The POINT= option can be used for accessing an observation directly in an uncompressed data set.
Example: The following program creates data set exam.result1 from the data set exam.result2. This program accesses the 5th observation directly from the SAS data set. Number is a temporary variable that is created and contains the observation number of observation to be read. It is assigned a value before the set statement is executed. The output statement is used to override the automatic output and write this observation directly to the data set. The stop statement is used for preventing continuous looping.

```
data exam.result1 ;
    number=5;
        set exam.result2 point=number;
    output;
    stop;
run;
```

35: Which option is used for controlling direct access in a compressed data set?
Answer:
The POINTOBS = option can be used controlling whether direct access is allowed in a compressed data set.
Example: The following program creates a compressed data set exam.result1 from the data set exam.result2. The option pointobs=yes ensures that random access to the compressed data set exam.result1 is allowed.

data exam.result1 (compress= YES pointobs= yes);
    set exam.result2;
run;

36: Once a SAS data file is compressed, is it possible to change the setting to uncompressed?
Answer:
Once a data file is compressed the settings become a permanent attribute of the file. The file has to be created again to change the setting to uncompressed.

37: Explain the significance of REUSE= option.
Answer:
REUSE= option is used to specify whether SAS reuses the space when observations get added to the compressed data set. If the reuse= system option is set to YES, then SAS tracks and reuses the free space in the compressed data set which is created.
Example: The following program creates a compressed data set exam.result1 from the data set exam.result2. Since the option reuse= is set to yes SAS tracks and reuses the free space in the exam.result1 data set.

data exam.result1 (compress= YES reuse= yes);
    set exam.result2;
run;

38: What is the main difference between a SAS data file and a SAS data view?
Answer:
SAS data file and SAS data view are both SAS data sets. The main difference is that SAS data file contains both descriptor information and data values. (Descriptor information refers to the details of the data set like name of the data set, number of observations, number of variables, attributes of variables.) The data view contains only descriptor information about the data and does not contain the values. The data view also contains information about how to retrieve the data.

39: What are the sources from which SAS data view can extract the data?
Answer:
SAS data view can extract the data from a variety of sources, namely a raw data file, SAS data file, PROC SQL views, SAS/access View, DB2, Oracle, or any other DBMS data.

40: What are the main advantages of using a data step view?
Answer:
The main advantages of using a data step view are as follows:
   a) Creating a data step view always helps to conserve disk space by avoiding storing of large data files several times
   b) It is always possible to access the most recent data
   c) It helps in combining the data from multiple sources

41: Explain how to create a data step view.
Answer:
To create a data step view, use the option view= after the name of the view in the data step.
Example: The following example program creates a view exam.resultview from the file that is referenced by the fileref result. The view= option tells SAS to compile the program and store the program.

```
data exam.resultview / view=exam.resultview;
    infile result;
run;
```

42: How do you check the source statement related to a DATA step view?
Answer:
The source statement related to a DATA STEP VIEW can be retained by using the describe statement. The describe statement writes a copy of the source code to SAS log.
Example: The following example uses describe statement to write the source code of the view exam.resultview to sas log.

```
data view=exam.resultview;
    describe;
run;
```

43: Is the code submitted to create a DATA STEP view executed?
Answer:
No. When a data step view is created, the data step is partially compiled and the code is stored in the SAS library with a member type of view.
Example: The following example program is used to create a view exam.resultview from the file that is referenced by the fileref result. The view= option tells SAS to compile the program and not execute. This code is then stored in the library referenced by the libref exam.

```
data exam.resultview / view=exam.resultview;
    infile result;
run;
```

44: What happens when a DATA STEP view is referenced in a proc step?
Answer:
When a data step view is referenced in a proc step, the

intermediate code that was generated during the creation of the view is located. This intermediate code is then resolved and executable code is generated for the host environment. The generated code is executed as the proc step requests for information. A data step view is referenced in the same way as any other SAS data set is referenced.
Example: The following program illustrates how a view exam.resultview is referenced by a proc print step.

proc print data =exam.resultview;
run;

45: Which of these methods is more efficient when the required data is used repeatedly in a program - creating a data set or creating a data step view?
Answer:
When there is a requirement to use the same data repeatedly then creating a temporary data set is more efficient than creating a data step view. Instead of referencing a data view in each step, it is preferable to create a temporary data file and read the data view into it. Then the temporary data set can be referenced in the subsequent steps. Then the temporary file can be referenced rather than referencing a data view, thus enabling SAS to execute the data view only once instead of three times.
Using a data set has one more advantage over the data step view. If there is any change to the raw data file while the code is running, the results will be inconsistent unless you have created a SAS data set file.

46: How does a SAS DATA STEP VIEW handle multiple passes through the data?
Answer:
When a SAS DATA VIEW is used with a procedure that requires multiple passes through the data the view builds a cache, referred to as spill file. This spill file contains all the required observations. SAS reads the data in the spill file on each of the passes through

the data to ensure that the same data is read in all the passes.

47: How does the updating of observations differ in compressed data files and uncompressed data files?
Answer:
In uncompressed data files each observation occupies the same number of bytes. New observations are added at the end of the file. If new observation will not fit on last page a new page is added.

Compressed data files treat an observation as a single string of bytes and ignore variable types and boundaries. The observations are different in length. An updated observation is stored on the same page and uses the available space. If enough space is not available, then observation is stored on next page with enough space and a pointer is stored on the original page.

48: What is the default size of view buffer?
Answer:
The default size of the view buffer is 32k. The number of observations that can be read into the view buffer depends on observation length. If the observation length is larger than 32k, then only one observation can be read into the buffer at a time.

This page is intentionally left blank

Best Practices

49: What is the best practice to follow while sub-setting the data?
Answer:
While creating a subset of the data, care must be taken to position the sub-setting if statement in the data steps as soon as logically possible in order to save most of the resources.
Example: The following examples create a data set exam.result1 from the data set exam.result2.
In this program the sub-setting condition is placed at the bottom of the data step. Here the variables total & year are calculated for all observations. But since the sub-setting condition is placed at the bottom only those observations whose result is distinction is written to the output data set exam.result1.

```
libname exam 'c:\myprog';
data exam.result1;
    set exam.result2;

    total = marks1+marks2+marks3;
    year = year(ExamDate);
    if result = 'distinction';
run;
```

In this program the sub-setting condition is placed at the top of the data step. Here the variables total & year are calculated for only those observations whose result is distinction. This results in saving a lot of resources like CPU TIME, disk storage and data storage space.

```
libname exam 'c:\myprog';
data exam.result1;
    set exam.result2;
    if result = 'distinction' then
    do;
        total = marks1+marks2+marks3;
        year = year(ExamDate);
```

       end;
run;

50: When is the IF-THEN/ELSE statement more used and what best practices should be followed?
Answer:
The use of IF-THEN/ ELSE statement is more effective when:
   a) There are only a few conditions to check
   b) The data values are character values
   c) The distribution of the values is not uniform

The best practices to be followed while using IF- THEN/ ELSE statement are as follows:
   a) The most frequently occurring condition is checked first and continue checking in the decreasing order of frequency
   b) When multiple statements are to be executed based on a condition then it is advised to put the statements in a DO group
   c) Avoid using parallel IF statements and incorporate ELSE IF condition. The use of parallel IF statement requires each condition to be checked and executed. While using ELSE IF, if the true condition is found subsequent statements are not executed. This results in saving the system resources

Example: The following program example creates a data set exam.result1 from the data set exam.result2. Here the majority of values of the variable result falls into the category of distinction so that condition is checked first. Then conditions are checked in the decreasing order of frequency. When a condition is true, multiple statements are to be executed so the statements are put in a do loop. ELSE IF is used so that while processing an observation if the true condition is found subsequent conditions are not checked for that observation.

libname exam 'c:\myprog';

```
data exam.result1;
    set exam.result2;
    if result = 'distinction' then
    do;
        total = marks1+marks2+marks3;
        year = year(ExamDate);
        level= 1;
    end;
    else if result = 'first class' then
    do;
        total = marks1+marks2+marks3;
        year = year(ExamDate);
        level= 2;
    end;
    else
    do;
        total = marks1+marks2+marks3;
        year = year(ExamDate);
        level= 3;

    end;
run;
```

51: When is the SELECT statement more suitable and what are the best practices to be followed while employing it?
Answer:
The SELECT statement is more effective when:
    a) There are many conditions to check
    b) The distribution of the data values is uniform

The best practices to be followed while using SELECT statement are as follows:
    a) The most frequently occurring condition is checked first and continue checking conditions in decreasing order of frequency
    b) When multiple statements are to be executed based on a

condition then it is advised to put the statements in a DO group

Example: The following program creates a data set exam.result1 from the data set exam.result2. Here the majority of values of the variable result falls into the category of distinction so that condition is checked first. Then conditions are checked in the decreasing order of frequency. When a condition is true, multiple statements are to be executed so the statements are put in a do loop.

```
libname exam 'c:\myprog';
data exam.result1;
    set exam.result2;
    select( result);
    when ('distinction') then
    do;
        total = marks1+marks2+marks3;
        year = year(ExamDate);
        level= 1;
    end;
    when ('first class') then
    do;
        total = marks1+marks2+marks3;
        year = year(ExamDate);
        level= 2;
    end;
otherwise;
do;
    total = marks1+marks2+marks3;
    year = year(ExamDate);
    level= 3;

    end;
run;
```

52: List the best practices while calling a function.

Answer:
The best practice while using function is to write program in such a way that the function is called minimal number of times rather than repetitively using the same function in many SAS statements. Even though the uses of SAS functions are convenient, they are very expensive in terms of CPU resources.

Example: The following programs create a data set exam.result1 from the data set exam.result2. This example illustrates the concept of reducing the number of calls made to the function. In the following program the year function is executed many times.

```
libname exam 'c:\myprog';
data exam.result1;
    set exam.result2;
    if year(ExamDate) = 2000 then level= 00;
    else if year(ExamDate) = 2001 then level= 01;
    else if year(ExamDate) = 2002 then level= 02;
    else if year(ExamDate) = 2003 then level= 03;
    else if year(ExamDate) = 2004 then level= 04;
    else if year(ExamDate) = 2005 then level= 05;
    else if year(ExamDate) = 2006 then level= 06;
run;
```

In the following program the year function is called only once and is more efficient.

```
libname exam 'c:\myprog';
data exam.result1;
    set exam.result2;
    year1= year(ExamDate);
    if year1 = 2000 then level= 00;
    else if year1 = 2001 then level= 01;
    else if year1 = 2002 then level= 02;
    else if year1 = 2003 then level= 03;
```

```
      else if year1 = 2004 then level= 04;
      else if year1 = 2005 then level= 05;
      else if year1 = 2006 then level= 06;
run;
```

53: Which best practice needs to be followed while creating multiple subsets of a SAS data set?

Answer:
The best practice that needs to be followed while creating multiple subsets of a SAS data set is to use a single data step. This saves the resources as the input data is read only once.
Example: This example illustrates the benefits of using a single data step versus using a series of data steps.
The following program illustrates the use of multiple data steps and reads the data 3 times from the data set exam.result2.
Individual IF statements appear in 3 data steps.

```
libname exam 'c:\myprog';
data exam.distinction;
    set exam.result2;
    if result = 'distinction';
run;
data exam.fclass;
    set exam.result2;
    if result = 'First Class';
run;
data exam.nclass;
    set exam.result2;
    if result = 'No Class';
run;
```

The following program illustrates the use of a single data step and reads the data only one time from the data set exam.result2. Individual IF statements appear in 3 data steps. The following program is more efficient as it helps in conserving system resources.

libname exam 'c:\myprog';
data exam.distinction exam.fclass exam.nclass;
    set exam.result2;
        if result = 'distinction' then output exam.distinction;
        else if result = 'First Class' then output exam.fclass;
        else if result = 'No Class' then output exam.nclass;
run;

54: Which best practice needs to be followed while using the SORT procedure to sort a SAS data set?
Answer:
The best practice that needs to be followed while using SORT procedure is to use a where statement in the procedure rather than creating a subset and sorting the data.
Example: The following programs create a data set exam.result1 from the data set exam.result2. This example illustrates the benefits of using a where statement in sort procedure against using a data step to subset and then sort the data.
The following program creates a data set exam.result1 from the data set exam.result2 by subsetting the observations based on the value of the variable result. The second step sorts the data. This method requires two passes through the data- first to subset the data and second to sort the data. This results in the improper utilization of system resources.

libname exam 'c:\myprog';
data exam.result1;
    set exam.result2;
    where result in ('distinction', 'First Class', 'No Class') ;
run;
proc sort data = exam.result1;
    by result;
run;

The following program illustrates the use of the where statement in a proc sort. This produces a result identical to the one produced by the above program. The following program is more efficient as it helps in conserving system resources.

libname exam 'c:\myprog';
proc sort data = exam.result2 out=exam.result1;
    by result;
    where result in ('distinction', 'First Class', 'No Class') ;

run;

55: What best practice needs to be followed to change the attribute of a variable?
Answer:
The best practice needing to be followed while changing the attribute of a variable is to use PROC DATASETS rather than using a DATA STEP. This conserves resources.
Example: The following programs create a data set exam.result1 from the data set exam.result2. This example illustrates the benefits of using a where statement in sort procedure against using a data step to subset and then sort the data.
The following program reads the data set exam.result1. A rename statement is used in a data step to rename the variable result to Final Result. This results in excessive utilization of system resources.

libname exam 'c:\myprog';
data exam.result1;
    set exam.result1;
    rename result = Final Result ;
run;

The following program illustrates the use of the proc datasets procedure. This produces the result identical to the one produced by the above program. However the following program is more efficient and conserves system resources.

```
libname exam 'c:\myprog';
proc datasets lib = exam nolist;
    modify result1;
        rename result = Final result;
quit;
```

56: While subsetting the observations is the – IF statement or Where statement more efficient?

Answer:
The purpose of both the if statement and the where statement is to check the specific condition to proceed with the processing of observation. But a where statement is more efficient than the if statement.

The where statement selects the observations from the input buffer before they are loaded into the program data vector which results in saving the CPU time. The if statement loads all the observations into the program data vector. If the condition is found to be true then the observation is processed and written to the output buffer.

Example: The following program illustrates the use If statement.

```
libname exam 'c:\myprog';
data exam.distinction;
    set exam.result2;
        if result = 'distinction';
run;
```

The following program illustrates the use of the Where statement. Even though the below program produces the same result as above program, the use of the Where statement is more efficient in terms of CPU resources.

```
libname exam 'c:\myprog';
data exam.distinction;
    set exam.result2;
        where result = 'distinction';
```

run;

57: How does the scope of selection of data differ in terms of IF statement and WHERE statement?
Answer:
The if statement selects the records from external files, observations from data sets, observations created with input statement, and observations based on the values of computed variables.
The Where statement can select the observations only from the input SAS data sets.

58: Which best practice needs to be followed while subsetting the data read from an external file?
Answer:
The best practice which needs to be followed while creating a subset of data read from an external file is to read selected variable first and then subsetting the data. This helps in saving the CPU time compared to reading all the variables and then creating a subset
Example: The following program reads all the variables from the external file referenced by the fileref distinction. Then it creates based on the value of the variable result. Only those observations which have the value of distinction for the variable result is written to the data set exam.distinction.

```
data exam.distinction;
    infile distinction;
    input @1 slno 2.
        @3 name $13.
        @16 marks 3.
        @19 Address $20.
        @39 subjects $20.
        @59 result $20;
    if result = 'distinction';
run;
```

The following program reads the variable result from the external file referenced by the fileref distinction and holds the input buffer using the single trailing (@) sign. Then the if statement is used to check the value of the variable result. If the value of the variable result is not equal to distinction then the values of other variable are not read or written to the output data set.

```
data exam.distinction;
    infile distinction;
        input @59 result $20. @;
            if result = 'distinction' ;
            input @1 slno 2.
                @3 name $13.
                @16 marks 3.
                @19 Address $20.
                @39 subjects $20.
                @59 result $20;
run;
```

59: How does the positioning of DROP= and KEEP= data set option affect the resource usage?
Answer:
The positioning of DROP= and KEEP= data set option can affect the resource usage. When DROP= and KEEP= data set option is mentioned in the set statement it affects the variables read into the program data vector. Reading only those variables that need to be processed in the data step can improve the resource usage. When the DROP= and KEEP= data set options are used in the data statement, the affects which variables are being written to the output data set.

Example: The following program reads all the variables from the data set exam.result2 and creates a data set exam.result1. Here all the variables are read from the input data set. This results in considerable waste of system resources.

```
data exam.result1 (drop= subjects address);
```

```
    set exam.result2;
    input @1 slno 2.
        @3 name $13.
        @16 marks1 3.
        @19 marks2 3.
        @22 subjects $20.
        @42 result $20
        @62 address $30;
    if result = 'distinction';
        total= marks1+ marks2;
run;
```

The following program also reads the data from the data set exam.result2 and creates a data set exam.result1. Here only those variables required for further processing are read from the input data set. This helps in conserving the system resources as only required variables are written into the program data vector.

```
data exam.result1;
    set exam.result2 (drop= subjects address);
    input @1 slno 2.
        @3 name $13.
        @16 marks1 3.
        @19 marks2 3.
        @22 subjects $20.
        @42 result $20
        @62 address $30;
    if result = 'distinction';
        total= marks1+ marks2;
run;
```

60: Which method helps in optimizing performance of a SAS program in regard to the storage of data?
Answer:
The method that helps in optimizing the performance with regard to the storage of data is to create a SAS data set to store the data

rather than reading from an external file if SAS used to repeatedly analyses the data. Even though SAS data sets are larger than external files, reading from the sas data sets saves the CPU time when compared with reading from an external file.

Another advantage of storing the data in a SAS data set is that SAS data sets contains useful information like the data set attributes, observations, variable attributes, etc. Any function or SAS procedure can be applied to data in the SAS data set without further conversion.

61: Use an example to explain run group processing.
Answer:
RUN: group processing is an effective way to end unnecessary procedure invocation. RUN-group processing is associated with those procedures that can accomplish multiple tasks with a single procedure invocation: Eg. Proc data sets.

The proc datasets can use run-group processing to process sets of statements without ending the procedure.

Example: The following example illustrates run-group processing. This shows how the datasets procedure is used to modify two data sets - result1 & result2 with one procedure invocation. When the proc datasets executes, SAS reads the statements associated with the first task that is modifying the dataset result1 until it reaches the run statement. SAS executes all the preceding statement and then continues reading until it reaches second run statement. Then the previous step is executed. PROC DATASETS is terminated using the quit statement.

```
proc datasets lib= exam nolist;
modify result1;
    rename result= final result;
    label date = 'Exam Date';
run;
modify result2;
    format date date9.;
run;
```

quit;

62: Explain the NOLIST option.
Answer:
The NOLIST option is used along with proc datasets to suppress the printing of library contents to SAS log. This helps in saving I/O resources.

Example: In the following example the datasets procedure modifies two data sets – result1 & result2 with one procedure invocation. The NOLIST option is used to suppress the printing of contents of SAS library (the details of other members of the library exam) to SAS log there by conserving the I/O resources.

```
proc datasets lib= exam nolist;
modify result1;
    rename result= final result;
    label date = 'Exam Date';
run;
modify result2;
    format date date9.;
run;
quit;
```

This page is intentionally left blank

Sorting Strategies

63: Is there any way to avoid the use of PROC SORT by using an index?
Answer:
An index can be used along with by group processing to avoid the use of proc sort. By group processing helps in processing the observations from one or more data sets grouped by the values of common variable. When by group processing is used with an index based the by variables, the use of sort procedure can be avoided. Even if there are changes in the data, there is no need to resort it as the indexes get updated on its own.
Example: The following example shows the examples of usage of by group processing with an index. The data set exam.result1 is indexed on the variable, author.

```
data _null_;
    set exam.result1;
    by author;
run;
```

In the following program the data set exam.result1 is sorted by using proc sort. Then the data is read by using data step. The results produced by both programs are identical.

```
proc sort data = exam.result1;
    by author ;
run;
data _null_;
    set exam.result1;
    by author;
run;
```

64: What are the main disadvantages of using BY-group processing with an index?
Answer:
The main disadvantages of using by-group processing with an index are as follows:

a) This requires storage space for index which results in more utilization of disk space
b) It is less efficient than sequentially reading a sorted data set as this requires retrieving the entire file to process the data

65: Which option can be used with the by statement to create ordered or grouped reports without sorting the data?
Answer:
The NOTSORTED option can be used with a BY statement to create ordered or grouped reports without sorting the data. This produces the result in which the observations which are having the same value for the BY variables are grouped together but not sorted in the alphabetical or numerical order.
Example: Consider a data set exam.result1 which has the values sorted by the variable result. Now if you wish to have a report ordered by the values of another variable author, you need not sort the data again. The option notsorted can be used with the by statement to produce the result. The output is grouped by the values of the variable author

proc print data = exam.result1;
    by author notsorted ;
run;

66: The NOTSORTED option cannot be used with what two statements?
Answer:
The NOTSORTED option cannot be used along with merge and update statements.

67: Is it allowed to use the NOTSORTED option along with the temporary variables – first.Variable & last.variable?
Answer:
Yes, it is possible to use the NOTSORTED option along with the temporary variables FIRST.Variable and LAST.variable.

FIRST.Variable and LAST.variable are temporary variables in the PDV and they identify the first and last observations in each BY group.
Example: The following program creates a data set exam.result1 from the data set exam.result2. SAS creates two temporary variables- first.subject &last.subject. In the input data set the observations which are having the same values of subject (politics, material science, electromagnetic studies) is grouped together. When an observation is first in a by group, the value of first.subject is set to 1. Only the first observation from each by group is written to the output SAS data set.

```
data exam.result1;
    set exam.result2;
    by subject notsorted ;
    if first.subject;
run;
```

68: Explain the GROUPFORMAT option.
Answer:
The GROUPFORMAT option is used to determine the beginning and ending of BY group by using formatted values of the variable rather than internal values. The GROUPFORMAT option is available only in the DATA step and is useful when a format is defined for a group of data.
Example: The following lines of code create a format for the data.

```
proc format data = exam.result1;
    value myformat
        '01Jan2012' d – '01june2012' d= 1;
        '01July2012' d – '01Dec2012' d= 2;

run;
```

Using the notsorted option and groupformat, the following lines of code creates which contain the details of the starting value of each by group. The use of temporary variables prevent the creation of a new variable for processing the data.

```
data exam.result1;
    set exam.result2;
    format startdate myformat.;
    by startdate groupformat notsorted;
    where year(startdate)=2012;
    if first.startdate then count=0;
    count+1;
    if last.startdate;
run;
```

69: What statement other than BY statement can be used to avoid sort?
Answer:
The CLASS statement can be used in place of a BY statement to avoid sorting. CLASS statement can be used along with MEANS, TABULATE, SUMMARY & UNIVARIATE procedures.
Example: In the following program class statement is used to create a single report which includes the mean value of the variables marks1, marks2 & marks3 for each category of value of the variable subjects.

```
proc means data = exam.result1 mean;
    class subjects ;
    var marks1 marks2 marks3
run;
```

70: When is a CLASS statement preferred over a BY statement?
Answer:
The CLASS statement is more efficient than BY statement if the data cannot be sorted. When the data set cannot be sorted, then the use of CLASS statement saves resources like CPU time, memory and I/O usage.
Also, the layout of results produced by class statement and BY

statement differ. The CLASS statement produces a single report while by statement produces a separate report for each value of the by variable.

71: Explain the significance of SORTEDBY= dataset option.
Answer:
The SORTEDBY= dataset option is used to specify how the data is ordered in an input data set. This does not sort the data set but it sets the value of the sorted flag to yes.
Example: The following program creates a data set exam.distinction from an external file referenced by the fileref qset1. The external file is already sorted by the values of the variable result. When the data set is created, the sorted information is stored with it. If you attempt to resort the data, a message gets displayed in the log stating that data set is already sorted and no additional sorting is required.

```
data exam.distinction(sortedby=result);
    infile qset1;
    input slno 1-5 result $ 6-20. Subject $ 22- 35;
run;
```

72: What is threaded processing in SAS?
Answer:
The threaded processing enables SAS to work with a high volume of data efficiently and to use the hardware capabilities to the maximum. This allows a single SAS session to use multiple I/O channels. It also enables the use of multiple CPUs managing threads.
A thread is a single piece of executable code within a process. Threaded processing executes multiple threads in parallel by using multiple CPU's. Threaded jobs are completed in less time than if each task was processed sequentially.

73: What are the two common constraints on the performance of a SAS application?

Answer:
The two common constraints on the performance of a SAS application are:
   a) **Constraints on I/O:** The applications that are I/O bound have slower input or output delivery. This means that the application can process the data faster than the time it takes to deliver input (deliver the data to the application) and to deliver the output (deliver the data from the application)
   b) **Constraints on the CPU:** The applications that are CPU bound takes more processing time compared to the time it takes for I/O delivery

74: How does the SAS SPD engine support threaded I/O?
Answer:
The SAS SPD Engine (Scalable Performance Data engine) supports threaded I/O by dividing each data set into smaller pieces that is then distributed among number of disks. Even though the data set is partitioned among the disks it can still be referenced as a single data set. When a data set is read, then the data from these disks can be delivered simultaneously. Thus SPD engine can read very large data sets by using a thread for each partition of data. Thus the SPD engine helps in improving the performance of data sets that are I/O bound.

75: How can we improve the performance of CPU bound applications?
Answer:
The performance of CPU bound applications can be improved by using multiple threads. They can run in either one CPU or in multiple CPU's. The use of a thread enables SAS procedures to solve the problems of CPU bound applications. These procedures have the capability to execute multiple threads in parallel if the hardware supports threaded processing.
Example: PROC SORT, PROC SQL, PROC MEANS have been thread enabled.

76: How can you enable threaded sorting?
Answer:
Threaded sorting can be enabled by using the THREADS system option or procedure option.
Example: The following program sorts the data set exam.distinction by the variable author. Threaded sorting is enabled by using the THREADS system option. Since the threaded sort is enabled, the observations of the data set exam.distinction gets divided into temporary subsets of equal size. Then each subset is processed by different processors=. Finally, the sorted subsets are then interleaved to get the final data set.

options threads;

proc sort data = exam.distinction;
    by author;
run;

77: Explain the CPUCOUNT= system option.
Answer:
CPUCOUNT= system option is used to specify the number of processors available for processing by the thread enabled applications. This value is used by SAS to calculate the number of threads required.
Example: The following program sorts the data set exam.distinction by the variable author. The option CPUCOUNT= is specified to be 3 which indicates that three CPU's are available for processing.

options cpucount= 3;

proc sort data = exam.distinction;
    by author;
run;

78: What is the range of the option CPUCOUNT=?

Answer:
CPUCOUNT= system option can have values between 1 and 1024.

79: What formula is used to calculate the additional workspace required by PROC SORT?
Answer:
While sorting the data, the space required by SAS is equivalent to the space required for holding the two copies of data file plus an additional workspace.
The space required by the additional workspace can be calculated by the following formula
Space required in bytes = (key variable length + maximum observation length) * number of observation * 4.
Where Key variable length refers to the length of all key variables
Key variable length, maximum observation length, and number of observations can be obtained by checking the descriptor portion of the data set.

80: Which system option is used to specify the memory available to sort procedure?
Answer:
The SORTSIZE= system option can be used to specify the memory available for sort procedure.
Example: The following program sorts the data set exam.distinction by the variable author. The option SORTSIZE= is specified to be 650M, which indicates that 650Mega bytes of memory is available for proc sort.

options sortsize= 650M;

proc sort data = exam.distinction;
    by author;
run;

81: What happens when the space required by the workspace is greater than the value specified by SORTSIZE= system option?

Answer:
The SORTSIZE= system option is used to specify the memory available for sort, but if the space required by the workspace is greater than the value that is specified in the sortsize= system option, then it results in increasing the processing time as the following actions needs to be performed by the proc sort
  a) Creation of temporary utility files in the Work directory
  b) Then requesting memory up to the value specified by SORTSIZE=
  c) Finally, writing a portion of the sorted data to a utility file

The above steps are repeated until the whole data set is sorted. Then the sort procedure interleaves the data to create the final sorted data set.

82: Use an example to explain how to divide and sort a large data set using Interleaving.
Answer:
When there is insufficient memory to hold the second copy of the data set or to provide additional work space, the data set is considered too large to sort. Dividing the data set into smaller data sets, sorting the individual data sets, and interleaving the sorted data sets prove an efficient method to sort the large data sets.
Example: Consider the following example. The data set exam.results is divided into three sets using the options firstobs= & obs=. Three temporary data sets work.one, work.two & work.three are created to hold the sorted results.

proc sort data = exam.results (firstobs=1 obs=250000) out=work.one;
by date;
run;

proc sort data = exam.results(firstobs=250000 obs=500000) out=work.two;

by date;
run;

proc sort data = exam.results(firstobs=500000 obs=750000)
out=work.three;
by date;
run;

The following program then combines the three sorted subsets into a single data set.

data exam.sortedresults;
    set work.one work.two work.three;
by date;
run;

83: Can PROC APPEND be used for combining the sorted sub sets while sorting large data sets?
Answer:
Yes, PROC APPEND can be used to combine the sorted sub sets while sorting the large data sets.
Example: Consider the following example. The data set exam.results is divided into three sets using the year function and the where statement. Three temporary data sets work.one, work.two & work.three are created to hold the sorted results.

proc sort data = exam.results out=work.one;
by date;
where year(date) in (2001,2002,2003,2004);
run;

proc sort data = exam.results out=work.two;
by date;
where year(date) in (2005,2006,2007,2008);
run;

```
proc sort data = exam.results out=work.three;
by date;
where year(date) in (2009,2010,2011,2012);
run;
```

The following programs then combine the three sorted subsets into a single data set exam.sortedresult.

```
proc append base= exam.sortedresults
    data = work.one;
run;

proc append base= exam.sortedresults
    data = work.two;
run;

proc append base= exam.sortedresults
    data = work.three;
run;
```

84: While dividing and sorting large data sets, which of these uses less resources while re-creating the data sets from sorted subsets: Interleaving, appending or merging?
Answer:
Interleaving (concatenating the data sets with set statement) uses minimal resources to recreate the data sets from the sorted subsets while dividing and sorting large data sets.
Example: The following example illustrates interleaving. The data set exam.results is divided into three sets using the options firstobs= & obs=. Three temporary data sets work.one, work.two & work.three are created to hold the sorted results.

```
proc sort data = exam.results (firstobs=1 obs=250000)
out=work.one;
by date;
run;
```

```
proc sort data = exam.results(firstobs=250000 obs=500000)
out=work.two;
by date;
run;

proc sort data = exam.results(firstobs=500000 obs=750000)
out=work.three;
by date;
run;
```

The following program then combines the three sorted subsets into a single data set.

```
data exam.sortedresults;
    set work.one work.two work.three;
by date;
run;
```

85: Explain the TAGSORT option.
Answer:
The TAGSORT option is used for sorting large data sets. The TAGSORT option will store the by variable and the observation number (called together as tags) in temporary files. After completing the sorting, the by variable and observation numbers are used to retrieve the records from the input data set in the sorted way.

Example: The following example illustrates the use of the tagsort option. The use of the tagsort option causes the by variable, date, and the observation numbers to be stored in the temporary file in the workspace. Then these temporary files are sorted. Next these tags are used to retrieve the observations from the data set and the sorted data set is recreated.

```
proc sort data = exam.results tagsort;
by date;
run;
```

86: How does processing time used by TAGSORT option differ from the regular sort?
Answer:
TAGSORT always uses more processing time than regular sort as additional CPU time and I/O resources are used to save memory. The difference in the processing while using the TAGSORT option and regular sort increases if the data is completely out of order in by variable.

If the data is in order with regard to by variables, then the CPU Time and I/O resource used is less and hence lesser processing time is taken. But, however, it still takes more processing time compared to regular sort.

87: Explain the NODUPKEY option.
Answer:
A NODUPKEY option is used for eliminating those observations that have duplicate by variable values. When NODUPKEY option is used along with proc sort, the by variables for each observation is compared with previous observation written to the output data set. If there is a match, the observation with duplicate value of by variable is not written to the data set.

Example: The following example illustrates the use of nodupkey option. The use of nodupkey option causes each observation to compare the value of the variable id with value of id for previous observation. If it matches, the current observation is not written to the SAS data set.

proc sort data = exam.results nodupkey;
by id;
run;

88: Explain the NODUPRECS option.
Answer:
The NODUPRECS option is used for eliminating duplicate observations by comparing all the variable values with the values of previous observation in the output data set. If an exact match is

found, the observation is not written to the output data set.
Example: The following example illustrates the use of noduprecs option. The use of noduprecs option causes each observation to compare the value of all the variables with values of variables for previous observation. If it matches, the current observation is not written to the SAS data set. The point to be noted here is that while using noduprecs option, the comparison is not for by variables alone but for all the variables.

proc sort data = exam.results noduprecs;
by id;
run;

89: Which alias is used in place of NUDUPRECS?
Answer:
NODUP can be used as an alias in place of NODUPRECS.
Example: The following example illustrates the use of the noduprecs option. The use of the noduprecs option causes each observation to compare the value of all the variables with values of variables for previous observation. If it matches, the current observation is not written to the SAS data set. The point to be noted here is that while using noduprecs option, the comparison is not for by variables alone but for all the variables.

proc sort data = exam.results noduprecs;
by category;
run;

In the following program the alias nodup is used in place of noduprecs. The result produced by the program below is identical to the one produced by the above program.

proc sort data = exam.results nodup;
by category;
run;

90: Explain the significance of SORTDUP= system option.
Answer:
SORTDUP= option is used to control the method of processing of NODUPRECS. SORTDUP= option can have two values; LOGICAL or PHYSICAL. When the value of the option SORTDUP= is specified as physical, it removes the duplicates based on the all the variables in the data set. When SORTDUP= is specified as logical, the duplicates are removed after the processing of DROP= & KEEP= data set options.

Example: The following example illustrates the use of sordup= option. The use of noduprecs option causes each observation to compare the value of all the variables with values of variables for the previous observation. If it matches, the current observation is not written to the SAS data set.

In the following program the value of sortdup= option is specified to be physical, so here the duplicates are removed considering all the variables in the data set.

options sortdup= physical;
proc sort data = exam.results (keep = id author subject name book)noduprecs;
by id;
run;

In the following program the value of sortdup= option is specified to be logical, so the duplicates are removed after processing the KEEP= data set option.

options sortdup= logical;
proc sort data = exam.results(keep = id author subject name book) noduprecs;
by id;
run;

91: Explain the significance of the EQUALS sort procedure option.

Answer:
The EQUALS option is used to determine the order of observations in output data set. It is normally used with NODUPRECS or NODUPKEY and it affects which observations are removed.
Example: In the following program the value of equals' option is used. The use of nodupkey option causes the elimination of observations with the same by variable value. Since the option equals is used, the order of observations remain the same in both input data set and output data set. NOEQUALS do not preserve the same order in the output data set.

proc sort data = exam.results nodupkey equals;
by id;
run;

92: Which option among EQUALS & NOEQUALS is the default and which saves CPU resources?
Answer:
The EQUALS option is the default and NOEQUALS helps in saving the CPU time and memory resources sincethe same order does need not be preserved in the output data set as in the input data set.
Example: In the following program the value of equals option is used. The use of nodupkey option causes the elimination of observations with the same by variable value, id. Since the option equals is used, the order of observations remain same in both input data set and output data set.

proc sort data = exam.results nodupkey equals;
by id;
run;

In the following program the value of noequals option is used. NOEQUALS does not preserve the same order in the output data set. This results in saving CPU resources and memory.

```
proc sort data = exam.results nodupkey noequals;
by id;
run;
```

93: Illustrate the use of FIRST Processing in the DATA step to remove the duplicate observations from the dataset.
Answer:
FIRST.processing can be used in the data step to remove the duplicate observations from the data set. The following program illustrates the use of bfirst.processing.
Example: The following program sorts the data set exam.results by the variable author and produces the data set work.one.

```
proc sort data = exam.results out=work.one;
by author;
run;
```

The following program removes the duplicate observation by using by group and first.processing. This program selects only those observations whose value of the variable, author, is unique.

```
data exam.sortedresults;
    set work.one;
    by author;
if first.author;
run;
```

94: Explain the option SORTPGM=.
Answer:
SORTPGM= option is used to determine which sorting needs to be used by SAS.
Example: The following line of code is used to specify the SORTPGM= option.

```
options sortpgm= best;
```

proc sort data = exam.results;
by subject;
run;

When the sortpgm= option has the value best, then SAS chooses the sort facility. This is the default value.
When the sortpgm= option has the value host, then SAS chooses the host sort facility. This is the third party sort package which is only available in some operating environments.
When the sortpgm= option has the value SAS, then SAS chooses the SAS sort facility.

95: Explain the option SORTCUTP=.
Answer:
The SORTCUTP= option is used to specify the number of bytes above which the host sort utility needs to be used rather than SAS sort utility.
Example: The following line of code is used to specify the SORTCUTP= option.

options sortcutp= 0;

proc sort data = exam.results;
by author;
run;

The value of the option sortcutp can be specified in bytes, Kilobytes, Megabytes or Giga bytes. It can also have hexadecimal values.

96: What is the default value for SORTCUTP= option in the UNIX and WINDOWS operating environment?
Answer:
The default value of SORTCUTP= option is zero in both Unix and Windows operating environment. This means that the Host sort utility is never used and sorting is always done by SAS sort utility.

97: Explain the option SORTCUT=.

Answer:
The SORTCUT= option is used to specify the number of observations above those the host sort utility needs to be used rather than SAS sort utility.
Example: The following line of code is used to specify the SORTCUT= option.

options sortcut= 0;

proc sort data = exam.results;
by subject;
run;

The value of the option sortcut can be specified in bytes, Kilobytes, Megabytes or Giga bytes. It can also have hexadecimal values.

98: Explain the option SORTNAME=.

Answer:
The SORTNAME= option is used to specify the host sort utility that will be used when the value of SORTPGM= is best or host. Example: The following program is used to specify the SORTNAME= option. Here, when the number of bytes required exceeds 10000, then SAS uses best sort which means that SAS takes up sort utility mentioned in the sortname= option that is syncsort

Options sortpgm=best sortcutp=10000 sortname=syncsort;

proc sort data = exam.results;
by subject;
run;

99: Demonstrate with a program how SAS processes the observation when accessing the data sequentially using the

where statement.

Answer:
When accessing the data sequentially, SAS has to go through all the observations in the order in which they are stored in the data set.
Example: The following program creates a new data set exam.set1 which contains a subset of the data set exam.set2. This program uses a where statement to select all those observations for the value of the variable author is equal to Tim. There is no index defined and so SAS uses sequential access to the data.

```
data exam.set1;
    set exam.set2;
    where author = ' Tim';
run;
```

When the above program is read, SAS loads one page of the data set exam.set2 into the input page buffer. After that, all the observations are read from the input page buffer until the where condition is satisfied. So after finding the observation for which the value of the variable author is equal to Tim, SAS loads the desired observations to PDV. Then the observations are copied from the PDV to output buffer. This process continues until the output buffer becomes full. When the output buffer becomes full, the data is written to the output data set, exam.set1.

100: Demonstrate with a program how SAS processes the observation when accessing the data using the index along with where statement.

Answer:
While accessing the data using an index, SAS goes to the desired observation directly without reading other observations.
Example: The following program creates a new data set exam.set1 that contains a subset of the data set exam.set2. This program uses a where statement to select all those observations for the value of the variable author is equal to Tim. There is an index defined on

the variable, author.

```
data exam.set1;
    set exam.set2;
    where author = ' Tim';
run;
```

The use of an index enables us to access the directly but it utilizes much more CPU time and resources compared to reading the data sequentially.

When the above program is submitted, the index is loaded into a buffer. SAS performs a search on the index and places the index on the first entry that contains a qualified value. SAS searches for a page in the input data set exam.set2 that has the value associated with qualified value in the index. Then that page is loaded into input buffer. The observation is accessed directly by the record identifier and loaded into PDV. From the PDV, it is loaded into output buffer. When the output buffer is filled, it is written to the output data set, exam.set1.

Samples

101: How is a systematic sample from a data set created with a known number of observations?
Answer:
To create a systematic sample from a known number of observations, it is necessary to use point= option with set statement.
Example: The data set exam.result2 contains 200 observations. To create a data set exam.result1 by reading every 10th observation, use the point= option inside a do loop.
In the example program below the do loop assigns a value to the variable temp used by the point= option to select the observations from exam.result2. The output statement writes observations to SAS data set and the stop statement stops the data step from continuing the observations after each 10th observation.

```
data exam.result1;
    do temp= 1 to 200 by 10;
        set exam.result2 point=temp;
        output;
    end;
    stop;
run;
```

102: What option can be used to find the total number of observations in a data set?
Answer:
NOBS option is used with set statement to find the total number of observations in a data set. This is automatically assigned during the compilation when SAS reads the descriptor portion of the data file.
Example: The following example illustrates the use of the nobs= option. Here nobs= option is assigned the variable temp and SAS automatically assigns a value to temp during the compilation. This value can accessed any time during the execution of a data step.

```
data exam.result1;
    set exam.result2 nobs=temp;
run;
```

103: How do you create a systematic sample from a data set whose total number of observations are unknown?
Answer:
Use point= option along with nobs= option in the set statement to create a systematic sample from a data set whose number of observations is unknown.

Example: The number of observations in the data set exam.result2 is unknown. If needed, the data set, exam.result1 is created reading every 10th observation by using point= option along with nobs= option in the set statement.

In the example below the do loop assigns a value to the variable temp that is used by the point= option to select the observations from exam.result2. During the compilation of the data set exam.result2, SAS automatically assigns a value to the variable final, which is equal to the total number of observations in the data set exam.result2. The output statement writes observations to SAS data set and the stop statement stops the data step from continuing the observations after each 10th observation.

```
data exam.result1;
    do temp= 1 to final by 10;
        set exam.result2 point=temp nobs=final;
        output;
    end;
    stop;
run;
```

104: Explain the RANUNI function.
Answer:
RANUNI function is used to generate a random number. The numbers returned by the ranuni function are between 0 and 1 non inclusive.

Example: The following example illustrates the use of ranuni function. It creates a variable, identifier, and assigns a random value to it. The value is assigned to the variable, identifier, remains the same even if you submit the data step multiple times or in multiple SAS sessions.

```
data exam.random1;
    identifier = ranuni(10);
run;
```

105: How is it possible to increase the interval of the random number generator?
Answer:
Increase the interval from which the random number is generated by using the multiplier.
Example: The following example illustrates the use of ranuni function with a multiplier. Here it creates a variable, identifier, and assigns a random value to it. The value which is returned by the ranuni function is between 0 and 1. In order to increase the interval, the multiplier 20 is used. Now the value assigned to the variable identifier will be a random value between 0 and 20.

```
data exam.random1;
    identifier = ranuni(0) * 20;
run;
```

106: What function is used to create a random integer?
Answer:
The CEIL function isused to generate a random integer. The numbers which are returned by the ranuni function is between 0 and 1 and is a random number. The ceil function can be used along with ranuni function to generate a random integer.
Example: The following example illustrates the use of ceil function. It creates a variable, identifier, and assigns a random value to it. The ranuni function creates a random number and ceil function returns a random integer

```
data exam.random1;
    identifier =ceil(ranuni(10));
run;
```

107: What is the term used for the argument of a ranuni function?
Answer:
The argument of a RANUNI function is referred to as a seed. The value of a seed is always a non-negative integer and should be less than (2^31)-1.
Example: The following example illustrates the use of ranuni function. Here it creates a variable, identifier, and assigns a random value to it. The number 10, which is the argument of ranuni function, is refered to as seed

```
data exam.random1;
    identifier = ranuni(10);
run;
```

108: Is the output produced by the ranuni function replicable?
Answer:
The RANUNI function generates random numbers starting from seed. If the value of seed is positive, then it is possible to replicate the output using the same data step. But if the value of seed used is zero, then the output produced is not replicable.
Example: In the following example ranuni function creates a variable identifier, and assigns a random value to it. The value assigned to the variable identifier, remains the same even if you submit the data step multiple times or in multiple SAS sessions since the value of seed is 10, which is positive.

```
data exam.random1;
    identifier = ranuni(10);
run;
```

Here also ranuni function creates a variable identifier, and assigns a random value to it. The value assigned to the variable identifier, differs every time you submit the data step or in multiple SAS sessions since the value of seed is 0. Hence the output is not replicated.

```
data exam.random1;
    identifier = ranuni(0);
run;
```

109: What is a RANDOM SAMPLE with replacement?
Answer:
The RANDOM SAMPLE is a type of representative sample. It contains observations that are chosen on random basis from a data set.

When we are creating a random sample, one observation can appear multiple times, so there is a chance the same observation is selected more than once. Therefore, a random sample is created with replacement so that when SAS chooses an observation from the data set that is already present in the sample, it replaces the observation in the sample rather than appearing twice.

110: How is a random sample with replacement created?
Answer:
The RANDOM SAMPLE with replacement is generated by using the ceil and ranuni functions together to generate a random integer, which in turn is assigned as the value to the variable pointed to by option point=.

Example: In the following example the ranuni function and ceil function are used together to assign values to the variable temp which is pointed to by point= option. The nobs= option assigns a value equal to total number of observations to the variable total. The variable total is then used as a multiplier so that during each iteration of the do loop the probability of picking each observation remains the same. Since zero is used as a seed of the ranuni function, the output differs each time the data step is submitted.

```
data exam.random1(drop=i);
    do i= 1 to 25;
        temp = ceil(ranuni(0))*total;
        set exam.result1 point=temp nobs=total;
        output;
    end;
    stop;
run;
proc print data = exam.random1;
run;
```

This page is intentionally left blank

Using Indexes

111: Explain the purpose of using indexes.
Answer:
The data in a data set can be accessed directly by using indexes, which locates the observations directly. An index is created to specify the location of observations based on the values of one or more key variables. Indexes provide direct access to the data set and help to do the following:
   a) Locate the observations directly for faster processing of the program
   b) Helps in joining and modifying observations
   c) Returning small subsets of observations for where processing
   d) Helps by processing by returning observations in sorted order
   e) Used in table look up operations

112: Explain how to create an index at same time of data set creation.
Answer:
INDEX= data set option is used in the data step to create an index at the same time of the creation of a data set.
Example: The following example creates a data set exam.set1 from the data set exam.set2. INDEX= data set option is used to create a simple index on the variable subject.

data exam.set1(index=(subject));
    set exam.set2;
run;

113: How do you create an index on an already existing data set?
Answer:
An index can be created on an already existing data set by rebuilding the data set. However, rebuilding the data set is not an efficient method for managing indexes. The PROC DATASETS procedure can be used to create indexes on already existing data set. The MODIFY statement along with INDEX CREATE

statement helps in creation of an index on already existing data sets.
Example: The following example creates an index author on the variable author, on the exam.set1 data set.

proc datasets library = exam;
    modify set1;
    index create author;
quit;

114: Explain how to delete an index from a data set.
Answer:
PROC DATASETS procedure is used to delete indexes on an already existing data set. MODIFY statement along with INDEX DELETE statement helps in deletion of index from data sets.
Example: The following example deletes an index author on the variable, author, from the exam.set1 data set.

proc datasets library = exam;
    modify set1;
    index delete author;
quit;

115: Where is an index associated with a data set stored and under what name?
Answer:
An index associated with a data set is stored in the same library with the data set. Index file has the same name as the associated data set, but have a different member type. All the indexes associated with a particular data set are stored in a single index file.
Example: The index file associated with the data set exam.set1 also has the same name as the data set that is exam.set1, but it is of the member type index.

116: How is information obtained about the indexes associated

with a SAS data set?
Answer:
Information about index associated with a data set is stored in the descriptor portion of the data set. It is possible to use either contents procedure or proc data sets to list the information in the descriptor portion of the data set.
Example: The following example illustrates the use of contents procedure for listing the descriptor portion of the data set, exam.set1, which provides information about indexes.

proc contents data= exam.set1;
run;

proc datasets;
    contents data= exam.set1;
run;

117: How is an indexed data set copied to a new location?
Answer:
An indexed data set can be moved to a new location by using the copy statement in proc data sets. When copy statement is used in proc data sets to copy a data set, a new index file is created for the new data file.
Example: The following example illustrates the use of copy statement in data sets procedure for copying the file set1 from the library exam to the work library. This cause an index file to created for the file work.set1

proc datasets library= exam;
    copy out= work;
    select set1;
quit;

118: Explain the COPY PROCEDURE with an example.
Answer:
COPY PROCEDURE is used to copy data sets from one location to

another. When pro copy is used to copy a data set that has an index associated with it, a new index file is created automatically for new data file. If the move option is used along with copy procedure, the old index file (the file in original location) is deleted and rebuilt at new location
Example: The following example illustrates the use of copy procedure. This program copies the data set set1 from exam library to the work library.

```
proc copy copy out= work in= exam;
    select set1;
quit;
```

119: How is an indexed data set renamed?
Answer:
PROC DATASETS along with a change statement is used to rename an indexed data sets. This preserves the index and the name of index file gets automatically renamed.
Example: The following example illustrates the use of change statement with proc datasets procedure. This program renames the data set exam.set1 to exam.finalset.

```
proc datasets library= exam;
    change set1= finalset;
quit;
```

120: How is a variable in an indexed data set renamed?
Answer:
PROC DATASETS along with a rename statement can be used to rename variables in an indexed data set. This preserves any indexes associated with the variables.
Example: The following example renames the variable, writer, to author in the exam.set1.

```
proc data sets library= exam;
    modify set1;
```

```
    rename writer = author;
quit;
```

Combining Data Vertically

121: How is a FILENAME Statement used to combine raw data files?
Answer:
FILENAME statement is normally used to assign a fileref with a single raw data file. FILENAME statement can be used to concatenate raw data files by assigning a single fileref to the input raw data files.
Example: In the following program example the filename statement creates the fileref result, which references three raw data files: set1.dat, set2.dat, set3.dat. These three files are stored in C:\data directory. The Infile statement identifies the fileref and the input statement is used to read the data from three files as if reading from a single raw data file.

filename result("c:\data\set1.dat" "c:\data\set2.dat" "c:\data\set1.dat");
    data work.final;
    infile result;
    input id $ result $ author $ date : date9;
run;

122: Which procedure can be used to view the structure and content of raw data files?
Answer:
The FSLIST procedure is used to examine the structure and content of a raw data file.
Example: The following example displays the raw data file set1.dat which is stored in the c:\data directory

proc fslist file = c:\data\set1.dat;
run;

123: Explain the significance of the COMPRESS function.
Answer:
The COMPRESS function is used to remove the desired characters from a source string.

Example: The following example creates a data set exam.set1 from exam.set2. The program also removes the space from the values of the variable result, by using compress function.

```
data exam.set1;
    set exam.set2;
    result= compress( result , ' ');

run;
```

124: How is the APPEND procedure used to concatenate two data sets?
Answer:
The PROC APPEND is used to concatenate the data sets. It reads one data set mentioned with DATA= option. PROC APPEND concatenates the data set even if there are variables in the BASE= data set, which are not there in the data set mentioned in the DATA= option.
Example The following program concatenates the two data sets exam.set1 & exam.set2.

```
proc append base=exam.set1
    data=exam.set2;
run;
```

125: What happens while using append procedure if the data set mentioned in the DATA= option has more variables than the data set mentioned in the BASE= option?
Answer:
When the dataset mentioned in the DATA= option has more variables than the data set mentioned in the BASE= option of PROC APPEND, then the appending of data sets does not take place and a message is written to SAS log giving information about the variable/variables missing in the data set mentioned with BASE= option.
This problem can be rectified by using FORCE option with

append procedure.
Example: The following program concatenates the two data sets result.old & result.new. Here the number of variables in the data set result.new is more than the data set result.old. So the force option is used. In the absence of the force option the appending of data sets will not take place.

```
proc append base=result.old
     data=result.new force;
run;
```

126: While using append procedure, what happens if the data set mentioned in the DATA= option has variables longer than the variables mentioned in the BASE= option?
Answer:
When the dataset mentioned in the DATA= option has variables longer than the variables mentioned in the BASE= option, it is necessary to use the force option. This helps in appending the data sets, however the variables of the data set mentioned in the DATA= option will be truncated.
Example: In the following program the data sets exam.result1 & exam.result2 both have a variable author. The length of the variable i the data sets are different since it is 12 in exam.result1 and it is 25 in exam.result2. The force option appends the data sets but the value of the variable author, will be equal to the length of the variable in exam.result1 (12).

```
proc append base=exam.result1
     data=exam.result2 force;
run;
```

Combining Data Horizontally

127: Use an example to illustrate the use of IF- THEN/ELSE statement for combining the data from a table with hardcoded values.

Answer:
An IF- THEN/ ELSE statement proves to be helpful when to combine the data from a table with values that are not stored in the data set.
Example: Suppose a data set exam.result contains information about students. The data set exam.result contains a variable named ID that records each student's identification number. If needed to combine the data from exam.result with a list of student's birthdates that is not stored in a data set, use the IF-THEN/ELSE statement.

```
data exam.newresult;
    set exam.result;
    if IDnum=101 then Birthdate='31JAN1982'd;
    else if IDnum=202 then Birthdate='30AUG1984'd;
    else if IDnum=403 then Birthdate='23MAR198'd;
    else if IDnum=504 then Birthdate='17JUN1991'd;
run;
```

128: List the advantages and disadvantages of using IF-THEN/ELSE statement to combine the data.

Answer:
An IF- THEN/ ELSE statement is helpful to combine the data. The advantages of using IF-THEN/ELSE statement are as follows:
  a) It is easy to use and easy to understand
  b) DATA step can be used along with IF-THEN/ELSE statement and hence it is more versatile
  c) It can be used for combining the data even if the look up values are not stored in the data set. If the look up values are stored in the data set, the IF-THEN/ ELSE statement can be used to handle any relations between the data
  d) It can be used to retrieve a single value as well as multiple values

The disadvantages of using IF-THEN/ELSE statement are as follows:
a) It makes the program longer
b) It requires maintenance; in situations where there are a large number of look up values, the look up values change frequently, or the look up values are used in multiple programs, then the resources required for maintaining this technique are large making it unsuitable for use

129: How do you use an ARRAY statement to combine the data from a data set with a list of values?
Answer:
An ARRAY statement proves helpful when combining the data set with list of values.
Example: In the example below a data set exam.result contains information about students. The data set exam.result contains a variable named ID that records each student's identification number. To combine the data from exam.result with a list of student's birthdates that is not stored in a data set, use the array statement.
Here an array of birthdates is defined with initial values. Then an assignment statement is used to retrieve the values of birthdates from the array depending on the values of id.

```
data exam.newresult;
    array birthdates{201:204} _temporary_ ('31JAN1982'd
        "30AUG1984'd '23MAR1988'd '17JUN1991'd);
    set exam.result;
    date=birthdates(ID);
run;
```

130: State the advantages and disadvantages of using an ARRAY statement to combine data.
Answer:
The main advantages of using ARRAY statement to combine data are as follows:

a) Since arrays are referenced by position, it is possible to identify the elements of array by position or any other numeric value
b) Multiple values or numeric expressions can be used to determine the array element to be returned

The disadvantages of using ARRAY statement to combine data are as follows:
a) Requires a large amount of memory for loading the entire array
b) It is capable of returning a single value from a look up operation
c) Required to supply the dimension of the array at compile time

131: How is the format procedure used to combine the data?
Answer:
The following example illustrates the use of the format procedure to combine data.
Example: Suppose you have a data set exam.result that contains information about students. Also, exam.result contains a variable named ID that records each student's identification number. To combine the data from exam.result with a list of student's birthdates that is not stored in a data set, you can use the format. In the following example, proc format step uses a value statement to hard-code the values. Then the data step uses the put function to associate the values of the variable id with the format created. Then use an input function to convert the character values to numeric values and assign a format of date9. The result is assigned to the variable date.

proc format;
    value birthdate 201 = '31JAN1982'
        202 = '30AUG1984'
        203 = '23MAR1986'
        204 = '17JUN1991';

run;

```
data exam.newresult;
    set exam.result;
    date=input(put(ID,birthdate.),date9.);
run;
```

132: State the advantages and disadvantages of using the format procedure to combine the data.
Answer:
The following are the advantages of using format procedure to combine the data:
  a) There is no need to creating a new data set to combine the data
  b) Formats can be used to categorize the data; they have the ability to change the appearance of a report without creating a new variable
  c) It is possible to create multiple formats and use all of them in the same data or proc step
  d) Format procedure uses binary search, a rapid searching methodology, to look for the values
  e) If there are any changes in the values, then the correction needs to be made only at one place and all the programs using this format will be changed automatically

The disadvantages of using the format procedure are as follows
  a) The main disadvantage is that format procedure requires the entire format to be loaded into memory for binary search. This requires more memory compared to other techniques if there are more values.

133: What happens when the variables in the input data sets of a MERGE statement have the same name but are different type?
Answer:
While doing the match –merge of two input data sets, if the variables have the same name it is also required that they have the

same type as well. Otherwise error and warning messages are written to the SAS log and match merging fails.
Example: The following program shows an example of match merging. The two data sets- exam.result & exam.result2 are sorted by the values of the variable, id. Then the two data sets are merged to produce a new data set exam.newresult. Both the data sets have two variables in common; id & author. The data type of id is numeric in both the data sets and the data type of author is a character in both the data types. SO the match-merge works successfully.

proc sort data = exam.result;
by id;
run;

proc sort data = exam.result2;
by id;
run;

data exam.newresult;
    merge exam.result exam.result2;
by id;
    run;

134: State the advantages and disadvantages of using the match-merge procedure.
Answer:
The main advantages of using the match-merge procedure are as follows:
   a) Any number of data sets can be mentioned in the merge statement as long as all the input data sets have a common by variable
   b) It can be used to combine data sets of any size
   c) Multiple by variables can be used to combine the input data sets and multiple values can be returned
   d) It returns the matching and non matching values, so

appropriate data step techniques can be used to return the desired results

The main disadvantages of using the match-merge procedure are as follows:
a) When a merge statement is used to combine the data sets that have a many to many relationship, it may not produce accurate results. This is because the merge statement does not create a Cartesian product while combining the data sets. So once an observation is read it is never re-read. Thus, it produces inaccurate results
b) The by variables must be present in all the input data sets and must be of same name

135: Illustrate the use of PROC SQL to combine the data.
Answer:
The following example illustrates the use of proc sql to combine the data.
Example: The following program shows an example of proc sql to combine the data sets. The data from the two data sets exam.result & exam.result2 are selected on the basis of the values of the variable id.

```
proc sql;
create table exam.newresult as
    select result1.id, result1.author, result1.subject,
        result2.name,result2.profit
    from exam.result1, exam.result2
    where result1.id=result2.id;
    order by id;
quit;
```

136: What are the benefits and the disadvantages of using PROC SQL for combining the data sets? If any
Answer:
When using PROC SQL for combining the data sets there are

benefits as well as disadvantages.
The benefits of using the proc sql to combine the data sets are as follows:
  a) There is no need to sort the data or index the input data sets
  b) It is possible to combine multiple data sets using proc sql and combining of the input data sets are done even if there are no common variables across the data sets
  c) PROC SQL can generate data sets, views or reports using the combined data

There are certain disadvantages associated with proc sql as follows:
  a) The maximum number of data sets that can be combined using proc sql is 32
  b) It is difficult to implement complex logic using proc sql
  c) The resources utilised by the proc sql is more compared to other statements such as merge

137: What is the function of KEY= option
Answer:
The function of KEY= option is to use an index retrieve the observations from the input data set. It is used along with a SET statement. When a set statement with key= option executes, SAS uses the index mentioned to retrieve that observation whose key variable value matches the value from PDV.
Example: In the following code example the result.set1 data set has an index named author associated with it. The following SET statement uses the author index to locate observations in result.set1 that have specific values for author.
    set result.set1 key=author;
SAS uses the index author to retrieve an observation from result.set1.

138: Illustrate the use of an index to combine the data sets.
Answer:

The index can be used to combine the data sets as demonstrated in the following example.

Example: The below example illustrates the use of an index for combining the two data sets exam.result1 and exam.result2 into one output data set exam.newresult. During the compilation phase, PDV is created. During the execution phase, the values from the first observation of exam.result1 are read into pdv. When the second set statement executes, the key=option uses the index author to directly read the observation which matches the value in the pdv. SAS reads the observation and records into PDV again. This process continues through iterations until all the observations are read.

```
data exam.newresult;
    set exam.result1;
    set exam.result2 key=author;
run;
```

139: Illustrate the use of _IORC_ variable.
Answer:
IORC (INPUT/OUPUT Return Code) is an automatic variable created when KEY= option is used. It is used to determine if index search is successful or not. When the value of _IORC_ is zero, it indicates that SAS found a matching observation.

Example: The below example illustrates the use of an index, author, for combining the two data sets exam.result1 and exam.result2 into one output data set exam.newresult. If any unmatched observations are read then the resulting observation will be read into exam.errors.

```
data exam.newresult exam.errors;
    set exam.result1;
    set exam.result2 key=author;
if _iorc_=0 then do;
    final = sum(marks1, marks2, marks3);
    output exam.newresult;
```

```
end;
else do;
    _error_ = 0;
    output exam.errors;
end;
run;
```

Lookup Tables

140: Explain the significance of prefix= option while using PROC TRANSPOSE.

Answer:

The PREFIX= option in PROC TRANSPOSE is used to specify a prefix to be used for naming the transposed variables in the output data set.

Example: The following program transposes the data set exam.result and outputs the result to a new data set exam.newresult. Here the name of the transposed variable created will be Finalresult1, Finalresult2, and Finalresult3.

```
proc transpose data= exam.result
        out= exam.newresult
            name=Month
    prefix=Finalresult;
run;
```

141: What option can be used with PROC TRANSPOSE to change the variable names?

Answer:

The RENAME= option can be used with PROC TRANSPOSE to change the name of the associated variables.

Example: The following program transposes the data set exam.result and outputs the result to a new data set exam.newresult. Here the name of the transposed variables col1, col2 & col3 is renamed to Finalresult1, Finalresult2, and Finalresult3.

```
proc transpose data= exam.result
    out= exam.newresult(rename = (col1 = Finalresult1 col2 = Finalresult2
            col3 = Finalresult3))
        name=Month;
run;
```

Formatting Data

142: Explain the significance of the LOG statement.
Answer:
Log statement is used to specify the data that is to be recorded in the audit trail. There are three types of values that can be specified in the log statement - ERROR_IMAGE, BEFORE_IMAGE, and DATA_IMAGE. When ERROR_IMAGE is specified as YES, the updates that created an error are stored in the audit trail. When BEFORE_IMAGE is specified as YES, the audit trail contains entries before the update. When DATE_IMAGE is specified as YES, the audit trail contains entries after the update.
In the absence of log statement, all the entries are logged in the audit trail.
Example: The following program illustrates a log statement. The audit setting before_image is set to yes, so the before update record images gets stored in the audit trail.

```
proc datasets lib= exam;
    audit set1;
    initiate;
log before_image =yes;
quit;
```

143: Explain the significance of a PICTURE statement.
Answer:
A PICTURE STATEMENT is used for creating a template for formatting the numeric values. The template is a sequence of characters that are enclosed in quotation marks.
The following example illustrates the use of a picture statement. Here non-zero digit selectors (9.99) are used to specify the label.

```
proc format;
    picture amt
        0-2='9.99 less'
        2<-4='9.99 moderate'
        4<-<10='9.99 high'
        other='999 provide value';
```

run;

The following program shows the format applied to the variable, amount. So if the amount has a value 4 then it will be displayed as " 4.00 moderate" in the output report.

proc print data=exam.set1;
    format amount rainamt.;
run;

144: Explain the significance of DIRECTIVES.
Answer:
DIRECTIVES refers to those special characters used with a picture statement to format date, time or date/time values. Whenever a directive is used with a picture statement, it is required to specify the DATATYPE= option in the PICTURE statement.
Example: The following programs illustrate an example of a directive. The following lines of code create a format startdate. All of the values are included by using the keywords LOW and HIGH. Here all the values are given a label %0d-%b%Y.
%d is a directive used to specify the day of the month. The 0 indicates that if the day of the month is a single digit. It should be preceded by zero.
%d is followed by –
%b is a directive used to indicate the abbreviated month name.
%Y is a directive used to assign the four digit year values. Two spaces are also included within the quotes.
DATATYPE= option is given a value of date since it used to specify the format for a date.

proc format;
    picture startdate
        low-high='%0d-%b%Y ' (datatype=date);
run;

The following program applies above format, startdate, to the variable, date. So the values of the variable will be displayed as dd-mmmyyyy (22-AUG2012).

proc print data=exam.set1;
    format date startdate.;
run;

145: Explain the functionality of FMTLIB keyword.
Answer:
FMTLIB keyword is used along with proc format statement to display the list of all the formats in a catalog along with description of values.
Example: The following program illustrates the use of fmtlib keyword. Once the following program is submitted, all the formats listed in the library are listed.

libname library 'c:\data\examset';
proc format lib=library fmtlib;
run;

146: While using FMTLIB KEYWORD, is it possible to list specific format rather than entire catalog?
Answer:
While using FMTLIB keyword, it is possible to list specific formats rather than entire catalog by using SELECT and EXCLUDE statements.
Example: The following program illustrates the use of SELECT statements. When the program is submitted only the documentation for $result format is listed.

libname library 'c:\data\examset';
proc format lib=library fmtlib;
    select $result;
run;

147: How to copy a format from one catalog to another?

Answer:
To copy a format from one catalog to another, PROC CATALOG can be used with a copy statement.
Example: In the program below, the PROC CATALOG copies the $RESULT. format from the Library.Formats catalog to the Exam.Formats catalog. In the select statement the full name of catalog entry is given as result.formatc.

proc catalog catalog=library.formats;
    copy out=exam.formats;
    select result.formatc;
run;
quit;

148: How is a PROC CATALOG step used to list the contents of a catalog?
Answer:
PROC CATALOG along with contents statement can be used to list the contents of a catalog.
Example: The PROC CATALOG example step below prints the contents of the work.format catalog.

proc catalog catalog=work.formats;
    contents;
run;
quit;

149: How is a format assigned to a variable in an existing data set?
Answer:
PROC DATASETS is used to associate a format with a variable in an existing data set. This modifies the descriptor portion of a data set.
Example: The following example program modifies the data set exam.set1. The variable, result, is associated with the format $success.

```
proc datasets lib = exam;
    modify set1;
        format result $success ;
quit;
```

150: What is the function of FMTSEARCH= system option?
Answer:
FMTSEARCH= system option is used to tell SAS the location of formats. It specifies the name of the catalog where the format needs to be searched.
Example: Suppose the formats specified in the exam and result library need to be used for a particular program, The following specifies that SAS needs to search the format in the exam and result library.
options fmtsearch=(exam result);

151: Which libraries are searched for formats when a format is referenced?
Answer:
When a format is referenced, SAS searches the format in the following libraries- work.formats, library.format and the libraries referenced by the fmtsearch= option.
Example: When the below line of code is executed, SAS searches the libraries work.formats, library.formats , exam.format & result.format
options fmtsearch=(exam result);

152: Explain the significance of the FMTERR option.
Answer:
The FMTERR option is used to specify that when SAS is unable to find a specified format, an error message is generated and processing the step is stopped. FMTERR system option is in effect by default.
Example: In the following program the format $success is specified incorrectly as $sccess. If the option FMTERR is in effect, SAS stops processing as this format cannot be found. An error

message is written to SAS log.

```
proc print data = exam.set1;
   format result $sccess ;
quit;
```

153: Is it possible to create a format from a SAS data set? Explain with a program.
Answer:
Yes it is possible to create a format from a SAS data set. The data set which is used for creation of a format is called a control data set. A format is created from a SAS data set by using the CNTLIN= option.
Example: The following program creates a format from the SAS data set exam.set1 and stores it in the catalog library.formats.

```
proc format library= library.formats cntlin= exam.set1;
run;
```

154: What prerequisites need to be satisfied by a SAS data set so it qualifies as a control data set?
Answer:
The data set used for the creation of formats is referred to as a control data set. The prerequisite that needs to be satisfied to qualify as a SAS data set are as follows:
 a) The control data set should contain the following variables; the format name, range, or starting value of the range and label. If there is no stop value specified for the range, SAS will assume the start value to be equal to stop value
 b) The control data set should contain the variable specifying the type of values that are numeric or character
 c) If multiple formats are to be created then the control data sets must be sorted by format name

155: Which option is used for creating a SAS data set from a

format?

Answer:

CNTLOUT= option is used for creating a SAS data set from a format. When CNTLOUT= option is used, SAS creates a data set from a format which contains variables storing information about the format.

Example: The following program creates a data set exam.set1. The select statement is used to select the format $success. In the absence of select statement, all the formats in the library.format catalog will be used for creating the data set exam.set1.

proc format library= library cntlout= exam.set1;
    select $success;
run;

Tracking Changes

156: What happens when a data step is submitted to create a data set that is also mentioned in the SET statement?
Answer:
When a data step is submitted to create a SAS data set that is also mentioned in the SET statement, SAS creates another copy of input data set. The original data set is deleted by SAS after the completion of the execution. The new data set may contain a different set of variables than the original data set.
Example: The following program creates a data set exam.set1 from the data set exam.set2.

data exam.set1;
    set exam.set2;
run;

157: What happens when a data step is submitted to create a data set that is also mentioned in the MODIFY statement?
Answer:
When a data step is submitted to create a SAS data set that is also mentioned in the MODIFY statement, SAS does not create another copy of data set. The same data set is modified. Hence, the set of variables does not change when a SAS data set is modified by using the MODIFY statement. By using the modify statement it is possible to do the following:
    a) Update all the observations in the data set
    b) Update the observations located using the index
    c) Update the observations using the transaction data set

Example: The following program creates a data set exam.set1 from the data set exam.set2. All the observations of the data set exam.set2 are modified since the variable, sum, is multiplied

data exam.set1;
    modify exam.set2;
    sum = sum*.95;
run;

158: How is a master data set modified using a transaction data set?
Answer:
A master data set can be modified using a transaction data set with the help of a modify statement along with a by statement. The by statement is used to match the observations of transaction data set and master data set.
Example: The following program modifies the master data set exam.set1. The changes which are required are stored in the transaction data set exam.newset. The master data set exam.set1 is updated by the matching values of the variable id.

    data exam.set1;
        modify exam.set1 exam.newset;
        by id;
    run;

159: Is it necessary to sort the master data set and transaction data set before applying the MODIFY statement?
Answer:
No, it is not necessary to sort master data set or transaction data set before applying the modify statement. When modify statement is used to modify the master data set it reads the observation from transaction data set and uses dynamic where processing to find a matching observation in the master data set. Therefore, it is not necessary to sort any of the data sets. However, if the master data set or transaction data set is sorted it will reduce the processing overhead.

160: What happens when there are duplicate values of BY variable in the master data set or transaction data set?
Answer:
When there are duplicate values of by variable in the master data set, first observation among the duplicate values is updated as the where processing begins at the top of the data set.
Example: The following program modifies the master data set

exam.set1. The required changes are stored in the transaction data set exam.newset. The master data set exam.set1 is updated by the matching values of the variable author.
In the example below there are duplicate values of the variable, author, in the data set exam.set1. Only the first observation among the duplicate values of author will get updated according to the values of the transaction data set exam.newset.

```
data exam.set1;
    modify exam.set1 exam.newset;
    by author;
run;
```

When there are duplicate values of by variable in the transaction data set, duplicate values overwrite. As a result, the last duplicate value in transaction data set will get updated in the master data set.
Example: The following program modifies the master data set exam.set1. The changes required are stored in the transaction data set exam.newset. The master data set exam.set1 is updated by the matching values of the variable author.
In the example below there are duplicate values of the variable author, in the data set exam.newset. The last observation from the group of duplicate observations of exam.newset is the result in the master data set.

```
data exam.set1;
    modify exam.set1 exam.newset;
    by author;
run;
```

161: Explain the significance of the option UPDATEMODE=.
Answer:
UPDATEMODE= option is used with the modify statement to handle the missing values in transaction data set. Two possible values of UPDATEMODE= option are missingcheck and

nomissingcheck. Missingcheck is the default value of the option UPDATEMODE=.

When the value of UPDATEMODE= option is missingcheck, this prevents the values of transaction data set from replacing the values in the master data set unless they are special missing values.

When the value of UPDATEMODE= option is nomissingcheck, the missing values in the transaction data set are allowed to replace the values in the master data set.

Example: The following program modifies the master data set exam.set1. The changes required are stored in the transaction data set exam.newset. The master data set exam.set1 is updated by the matching values of the variable author.

The missing values of transaction data set can replace the values of master data set as the option updatemode= is set to nomissingcheck.

```
data exam.set1;
    modify exam.set1 exam.newset updatemode=nomissingcheck;
    by author;
run;
```

162: How the observations located by an index modified?
Answer:
Modify the observations located by an index by using the modify statement with key= option.

Example: In the example below the data set exam.set1 needs to be modified. The data set exam.set1 has a simple index on the variable author and has some incorrect values. The correct values are stored in the data set exam.newset. The index author, specified by the key= option, is used to update the matching observations in exam.set1. The value for the variable, marks, exam.set1 gets replaced with the values of the variable, newmarks, of the data set exam.newset.

data exam.set1;

```
        set exam.newset;
        modify exam.set1 key= author;
        marks=newmarks;
run;
```

163: How does an updating with INDEX differ from updating using the BY statement?

Answer:
Updating a data set with an INDEX differs from updating using a BY statement in the following ways:
   a) When using an INDEX to update a data set, it is necessary to specify the update you want while it is not necessary to specify the update when using the modify statement with BY statement.
   Example: The following program modifies the master data set exam.set1. The changes required are stored in the transaction data set exam.newset. The master data set exam.set1 is updated by the matching values of the variable author. Here the modify with BY statement is used for modifying the master data set. There is no need for specifying the update operation.

```
        data exam.set1;
            modify exam.set1 exam.newset;
            by author;
        run;
```

The below program modifies the data set exam.set1 by using an index defined on the variable author. It is specified that the values of the variable mark, needs to be replaced with the values of newmarks.

```
        data exam.set1;
            set exam.newset;
            modify exam.set1 key= author;
            marks=newmarks;
```

run;

b) When using MODIFY with BY statement to update a data set, automatic overlay of non-missing values occur, which does not happen while updating the data set with INDEX. While using INDEX to update a data set, each observation of the transaction data set should have a matching observation in the master data set. For an observation of a master data set, there are multiple observations in the transaction data set, only the first observation is used. The other observations will generate run time errors and will stop the data step.

164: While using an INDEX to locate the values to be updated, how are the duplicate values handled?
Answer:
When an INDEX is used to locate the values to be updated, the missing values are handled in the following way:
   a) When there are duplicate values in the master data set, only the first value is updated
   b) When there are duplicate values in the transaction data set there are two points to be considered
      i) If the duplicate values are not consecutive, SAS updates the master data set. It keeps on updating and the last value among the duplicate group is the result in master data set
      ii) If the duplicate values are consecutive, SAS performs a one to one update. Then it finds a non-match and data step terminates with an error

165: Is it possible to use an OUTPUT statement in a DATA step that contains a modify statement?
Answer:
Yes, it is possible to use an OUTPUT statement in a DATA step that contains a modify statement. This will override the default behavior of data step with the modify statement. When the output

statement is specified, then the current observation is written to the end of the data set.
Example: The example program below modifies the data set exam.set1 by using an index defined on the variable author. The transaction data set exam.newset contains a variable result. If the value of result is Success, then the observation is added to the end of the data set and if the value of result is Failure, then that observation is deleted from the data set exam.set1.

```
data exam.set1;
    set exam.newset;
    modify exam.set1 key= author;
    if result = 'Success' then output;
    else if result = 'Failure' then remove;
run;
```

166: What is _IORC_?
Answer:
IORC (INPUT OUTPUT RETURN CODE) is an automatic variable whose value is a numeric code that indicates the status of most recent I/O operation. It is created when modify statement is used with a by statement or key= option.

167: How can you create the INTEGRITY constraints using DATASETS PROCEDURE?
Answer:
INTEGRITY constraints can be created using IC CREATE statements with DATASETS procedure.
Example: The below program uses proc datasets to create a primary key constraint on the data set exam.set1. The IC CREATE statement creates a primary key constraint on the variable, author, which ensures that the values of the variable, author, are not null and unique.

```
proc datasets;
    modify exam.set1;
```

ic create pkclass= primarykey(author) ;
quit;

168: In what situations are integrity constraints enforced?
Answer:
Once INTEGRITY constraints are created, SAS enforces the constraints when ever data is modified in place. That is the integrity constraints are enforced when ever data is updated using
a) Data editing windows
b) Data step with modify statement
c) PROC APPEND
d) PROC SQL with INSERT INTO, UPDATE, SET statements

169: How can you view the INTEGRITY CONSTRAINTS created on a data set?
Answer:
INTEGRITY constraints created on a data set can be viewed by reading the descriptor portion of the data set. It is possible to view the descriptor portion of the data set by using a contents statement in datasets procedure.
Example: The following program example can be submitted to view the descriptor portion of the data set, exam.set1. The descriptor portion will have the information about all the integrity constraints of the data set.

proc datasets;
    contents data = exam.set1;
quit;

170: How is an integrity constraint removed from a data set?
Answer:
The IC DELETE statement can be used with proc data sets to remove an integrity constraint from a data set.
Example: The below program removes the integrity constraint pkclass from the data set set1 located in the exam library. After deletion a message is written to SAS log.

```
proc datasets lib= exam;
    modify set1;
        ic delete pkclass ;
quit;
```

171: What is an AUDIT TRAIL?
Answer:
An AUDIT TRAIL is an SAS file that logs modifications made to the SAS data set. An audit trail is a read only file and it should be stored in the same library as that of the data set it tracks.
Audit trail tracks the modifications made by
  a) Modify statement with DATA STEP
  b) VIEW Table window
  c) PROC SQL with update, delete or insert statements

172: How is an AUDIT TRAIL initiated?
Answer:
An AUDIT TRAIL can be initiated by using audit and initiate statements with datasets procedure.
Example: The below program initiates an audit trail on the data set exam.set1.

```
proc datasets lib= exam;
    audit set1;
        initiate;
quit;
```

173: How do you read the contents of an AUDIT TRAIL file?
Answer:
An AUDIT TRAIL file can be read by using any SAS procedure that reads data like proc print or proc contents. It is mandatory to use type= data set option with the SAS procedure.
Example: The following program uses proc print to read the contents of the audit trail file associated with the data set exam.set1

proc print data = exam.set1 (type = audit);
run;
The following PROC CONTENTS reads the audit trail file associated with the data set exam.set1

proc contents data = exam.set1 (type = audit);
run;

174: What are AUDIT TRAIL variables?
Answer:
AUDIT TRAIL variables are variables that store information about the data modifications. The name of the audit trail variables begins with the keyword AT.
The audit trail variables include:
   a) _ATDATETIME_: Contains information about date and time of modification
   b) _ATUSERID_: Contains information user id associated with a modification
   c) _ATOBSNO_: Contains information about observation number associated with the modification
   d) _ATMESSAGE_: Contains information about log message at the time of modification
   e) _ATOPCODE_: Contains code describing the type of operation performed
   f) _ATRETURNCODE_: Contains information about event return code

175: Explain the function of BEFORE_IMAGE audit setting.
Answer:
The BEFORE_IMAGE audit setting is used to control the storage of records before the update. When the BEFORE_IMAGE audit setting is specified as YES, a before update record image is stored. Example: The following program initiates an audit trail on the data set exam.set1. The audit setting before_image is set to yes, so before the update record images are stored in the audit trail.

```
proc datasets lib= exam;
    audit set1;
    initiate;
log before_image =yes;
quit;
```

176: Explain the function of ERROR_IMAGE audit setting.
Answer:
ERROR_IMAGE audit setting is used to control the storage of those record images whose update was unsuccessful. When ERROR_IMAGE audit setting is specified as YES, audit trail will store those records where an error occurred while updating. Example: The following program initiates an audit trail on the data set exam.set1. The audit setting before_image is set to yes, so before update record images gets stored in the audit trail. Also, the error_image is set to yes. So those records are also stored in the audit trail whose updating produced the error.

```
proc datasets lib= exam;
    audit set1;
    initiate;
log before_image =yes error_image = yes;
quit;
```

177: Explain the function of DATA_IMAGE audit setting.
Answer:
DATA_IMAGE audit setting is used to control the storage of record images after update. When DATA_IMAGE audit setting is specified as YES, audit trail will store the record images updated Example: The following program initiates an audit trail on the data set exam.set1. The audit setting after_image is set to yes, so the audit trail store the record images after an update. Also the error_image is set to yes. So those records are also stored in the audit trail whose updating produced the error.

```
proc datasets lib= exam;
```

audit set1;
initiate;
log after_image =yes error_image = yes;
quit;

178: What is a user variable in an audit trail?
Answer:
USER VARIABLES of an audit trail are those variables that allow the person who is modifying the data set to enter information about the modification. USER VARIABLES are created with USER_VAR statement in the audit trail specification.
Example: The following program initiates an audit trail on the data set exam.set1. Here two user variables are created; name & reason. The USER_VAR statement is used to create the user variable.

proc datasets lib= exam;
audit set1;
initiate;
user_var name $20 label = 'Name of the user who made the modification'
reason $20 label = 'Reason behind the change';
quit;

179: Is it possible to suspend an audit trail then resume after some time?
Answer:
Yes, it is possible to suspend an audit trail and resume after a while by using proc datasets. Proc data sets when used with additional statements like suspend is capable of suspending an audit trail and resuming after a while if necessary.
Example: The following program suspends the logging of the events to audit trail but it does not delete the audit trail.

proc datasets lib= exam;
audit set1;

```
    suspend;
quit;
```

The following program resumes the logging of the events to audit trail

```
proc datasets lib= exam;
    audit set1;
    resume;
quit;
```

180: How are audit trails deleted?
Answer:
An audit trail can be deleted using proc datasets with the terminate statement.
Example: The following program terminates the logging of the events to audit trail and deletes the audit trail. A message is written to the SAS log when an audit trail is terminated.

```
proc datasets lib= exam;
    audit set1;
    terminate;
quit;
```

181: When is a generation data set preferred over an audit trail?
Answer:
An audit trail can be used to track the modifications made to the data set in place. But if the data set is replaced, the audit trail is deleted. In this scenario a generation data set is preferred over an audit trail.
GENERATION data sets allow maintaining multiple versions of data set. A generation data set is created each time a data set is replaced. Each generation is stored as a part of the group. All the members in a generation group have the same name but a different version number.

182: How is generation data sets initiated?
Answer:
GENERATION data sets can be initiated by using GENMAX= data set option while creating or replacing a data set.
Example: The following program initiates generation data sets. The program modifies the data set, exam.set1, and requests that up to 4 versions be kept.

proc datasets lib= exam;
    modify set1(genmax=4);
quit;

183: Name the scenarios where a generation data set is created.
Answer:
GENERATION data sets are created in situations where a data set is replaced due to modification. Some of these scenarios are as follows:
   a) Use of proc sort without OUT= option. This replaces the current data set
   b) Use of data step with set statement
   c) Use of data step with merge statement
   d) Use of proc sql with create table statement

184: How are particular generations of a data set selected from a generation group?
Answer:
The GENNUM= data set option is used to select a particular generation of a data set from a generation group.
Example: The following program illustrates the use of GENNUM= data set option. This is an absolute reference to a generation data set.

proc print data = exam.set1(gennum = 4);
run;

185: Is it possible to rename the generation group once the

generation data sets are created?
Answer:
Yes, it is possible to rename the generation group or any members of the generation group after the generation data set is created by using the change statement with proc data sets.
Example: The following program uses the change statement to rename the data set exam.set1 to exam.finalset. The code below will replace the name of all generations of the generation group.

```
proc datasets lib= exam;
    change set1 = finalset;
quit;
```

186: Which statement is used to delete any of the generation data sets?
Answer:
A DELETE statement along with proc datasets enables the deletion of any generation data sets.
Example: The following program uses the delete statement in proc datasets to delete all the generation data sets associated with exam.set1.

```
proc datasets lib= exam;
    delete set1 (gennum = ALL);
quit;
```

187: Explain the significance of the keyword HIST.
Answer:
HIST keyword is used along with delete statement to delete the generation data sets. When the value of gennum option is specified as HIST, all the historical versions are deleted.
Example: The following program uses the delete statement in proc datasets to delete all the historical versions of generation data sets associated with exam.set1.

```
proc datasets lib= exam;
```

        delete set1 (gennum = HIST);
quit;

188: What procedures are commonly used to produce a detail report?
Answer:
PROC PRINT and PROC SQL are commonly used to produce a detail report. Among these procedures, proc print generally uses fewer resources (CPU and MEMORY) compared to proc sql.
Example: The following program uses the proc print to produce a detail report based on the exam.set1 dataset. This program uses fewer CPU resources and memory.

proc print data = exam.set1;
    var slno result author set;
run;

The following program uses proc sql to produce a detail report. The result produced by the below program is identical to the one produced above.

proc sql;
select slno result author set
    from exam.set1;
quit;

189: Compare PROC PRINT and PROC SQL in terms of resource usage while producing a sorted subset detail report.
Answer:
While producing a sorted subset detail report, proc print and proc sql have similar resource usage.
Example: The following program uses the proc print and proc sql to produce sorted subset detail report. The resource usage associated with both the procedures are the same.
In the program example below, proc sort is used for sorting and ordering the data set, exam.set1.

```
proc sort data = exam.set1;
    where author = 'TIM';
by result;
run;
proc print data = exam.set1;
    var slno result author set

run;
```

The following program uses proc sql to produce a sorted subset detail report. A where clause is used for subsetting and order by clause is used for ordering. The result produced by the below program is identical to the one produced above.

```
proc sql;
select slno result author set
    from exam.set1
    where author = 'TIM'
    order by result;
quit;
```

190: While producing a summary dataset with one or more class variables, what tools are to be used if there are a large number of distinct combinations of class variables?
Answer:
It is possible to use many tools for summarizing data for one or more class variables like PROC MEANS, PROC SUMMARY, PROC REPORT, PROC TABULATE, PROC SQL, DATA STEP WITH PROC SORT.
However, if there are a relatively large number of distinct combinations of class variables, it is always efficient to use PROC SQL or DATA STEP with PROC SORT. Relatively large numbers of class variables means that the summarized data set to be produced may contain more than 10% of observation compared to the original data set.
Example: The following program illustrates an example of proc

sql. The below program calculates the average value of marks for each result value

proc sql;
    select result avg(marks)
        from exam.set1
        where author = 'TIM'
        group by result;
quit;

191: Which summarizing tool is most efficient for a small number of distinct combinations of class variables while producing a summary data set?
Answer:
If there are small numbers of distinct combination of class variables, it is always efficient to use PROC MEANS or PROC SUMMARY or PROC REPORT or PROC TABULATE. A relatively small number of class variables means that the summarized data set to be produced may contain 10% or less than 10% of observation compared to the original data set.
Example: The following program illustrates an example of proc means. The example below will produce a report that displays the mean of marks for each type of result (class variable).

proc means data = exam.set1 mean maxdec=2;
    class result;
    var marks;
run;

192: Why is a TYPES statement used with PROC MEANS?
Answer:
TYPES statement is used with PROC MEANS to specify the combination of class variables used to create types. This combination of class variables is used for producing required statistics and grouping the data accordingly.
Example: The following program illustrates an example of type

statement with proc means. The program below calculates the values of average marks for two combination of class variable. A class statement always needs to be used along with type statement. Here the results are produced for two combinations of class variables as specified in the type statement. An output report is generated by this program.

```
proc means data = exam.set1 mean maxdec=2;
    class dept result author;
    var marks;
    type result* author dept*author;
run;
```

193: Why use NWAY option with PROC MEANS?
Answer:
NWAY option is used with PROC MEANS to specify the combination of class variables to be used. This combination of class variables is used for producing required statistics and grouping the data accordingly. It is necessary to use separate proc means step with nway option for each combination of class variables.

Example: The following program illustrates an example of NWAY option with proc means. The program below calculates the values of average marks for two combinations of class variables. A class statement will always need to be used. Here the results are produced for two combinations of class variables as specified. Two separate proc means steps need to be used with nway option to calculate the statistics.

This program generates an output data set as well as an output report. The statistics from the first proc means is stored in the data set exam.set2 while the statistics from the second proc means is stored in the data set exam.set3.

```
proc means data = exam.set1 mean maxdec=2 nway;
    class dept result;
    var marks;
```

```
        output out= exam.set2 mean= avgmarks;
run;

proc means data = exam.set1 mean maxdec=2 nway;
    class result author;
    var marks;
    output out= exam.set3 mean= avgmarks;
run;
```

194: Is using WHERE= option allowed with PROC MEANS?
Answer:
Yes, it is allowed to use where= option with proc means. WHERE= data set option is used along with proc means to specify the combination of class variables.
Example: The following program illustrates an example of where = data set option with proc means. The program below calculates the values of average marks for two combinations of class variable. A class statement always needs to be used to specify the combination of variables. This program generates an output report. Here the statistics are produced according to the value of _type_ variable that is for 3, 4.
When the variable, _TYPE_ has a value of 3 then the statistics are generated for result* author. When the variable, _TYPE_ has a value of 4 then the statistics is a one-way table generated for dept.

```
proc means data = exam.set1 mean maxdec=2;
    class dept result author;
    var marks;
    output out= exam.set2( where( _type_ in (3, 4))) mean=
    avgmarks;
run;
```

195: How does the size of the subset to be extracted from a data set affect the decision to create an index?
Answer:

The size of the subset to be extracted is an important factor while deciding to create an index. It is always beneficial to create an index if a small subset of observations is to be retrieved from a large data file.

The resource usage associated with accessing the data with index is always higher compared to accessing the data sequentially. Index requires more CPU resources and Input output operations if the subset to be extracted is very large.

So the performance gain associated with an index becomes beneficial only if the subset to be extracted is very small. So SAS will use an index only if the subset to be extracted is less than 3% of the total data set. Also, if size of the subset is between 3 % and 33% SAS might use an index taking into consideration other factors as well.

196: Under what WHERE condition does SAS decide not to use an INDEX?
Answer:
SAS does not use an INDEX to process WHERE condition if it contains any of the following:
   a) Arithmetic operators (like +, -)
   b) Any function other than TRIM or SUBSTR (like MONTH, YEAR)
   c) Sounds like operator (=*)
   d) Variable to variable conditions (marks le criteria)
   e) SUBSTR function when searching from any other position other than 1st position like substr(identifier, 2)

In the above code, substr function searches from 2nd position.

197: What is compound optimization?
Answer:
COMPUND optimization is a process in which SAS uses a composite index to optimize the conditions on variables joined with logical operators. Multiple conditions on multiple variables are optimized through this method.

The prerequisites for compound optimization are as follows:
a) Where conditions must be connected by using AND expression
b) OR expressions are used if all the where conditions refers to the same variable
c) Where conditions must be having IN operator or EQ operator

198: Describe some situations in which compound optimization are not performed by SAS.
Answer:
COMPUND optimization is not performed by SAS if the where condition does not satisfy certain criteria. They are as follows:
a) IS NULL or IS MISSING
b) ANY FUNCTION
c) LIKE or NOTLIKE Operator
d) CONTAINS OPERATOR

199: Explain the CENTILES option.
Answer:
CENTILES option can be used to get the information about indexed variables. They store the details regarding the distribution of values for the variable. Centiles information can be obtained by using proc contents or contents statement.
Example: The following program illustrates the use of centiles option. This gives information about the centile information associated with exam.set1. This prints information about the distribution of indexed variables that helps in formulating where conditions to improve the efficiency.

proc contents data = exam.set1 centiles;
run;

200: How does the number of pages in a file affect the decision to use an INDEX?
Answer:

SAS decides about the use of an index after considering many factors including the number of pages in a file and order of data. SAS decides not to use an index if the total number of pages in the data file is less than 3. In this scenario sequential access is faster and more efficient in terms of resource use.

HR Questions

Review these typical interview questions and think about how you would answer them. Read the answers listed; you will find best possible answers along with strategies and suggestions.

1: What are the three most important things you're looking for in a position?

Answer:
The top three things you want in a position should be similar to the top three things the employer wants from an employee, so that it is clear that you are well-matched to the job. For example, the employer wants a candidate who is well-qualified for and has practical experience – and you want a position that allows you to use your education and skills to their best applications. The employer wants a candidate who is willing to take on new challenges and develop new systems to increase sales or productivity – and you want a position that pushes you and offers opportunities to develop, create, and lead new initiatives. The employer wants a candidate who will grow into and stay with the company for a long time – and you want a position that offers stability and believes in building a strong team. Research what the employer is looking for beforehand, and match your objectives to theirs.

2: How are you evaluating the companies you're looking to work with?

Answer:
While you may feel uncomfortable exerting your own requirements during the interview, the employer wants to see that you are thinking critically about the companies you're applying with, just as they are critically looking at you. Don't be afraid to specify what your needs from a company are (but do try to make sure they match up well with the company – preferably before you apply there), and show confidence and decisiveness in your answer. The interviewer wants to know that you're the kind of person who knows what they want, and how to get it.

3: Are you comfortable working for _____ salary?

Answer:
If the answer to this question is no, it may be a bit of a deal-breaker in a first interview, as you are unlikely to have much

room to negotiate. You can try to leverage a bit by highlighting specific experience you have, and how that makes you qualified for more, but be aware that this is very difficult to navigate at this step of the process. To avoid this situation, be aware of industry standards and, if possible, company standards, prior to your application.

4: Why did you choose your last job?
Answer:
In learning what led you to your last job, the interviewer is able to get a feel for the types of things that motivate you. Keep these professionally-focused, and remain passionate about the early points of your career, and how excited you were to get started in the field.

5: How long has it been since your last job and why?
Answer:
Be sure to have an explanation prepared for all gaps in employment, and make sure it's a professional reason. Don't mention difficulties you may have had in finding a job, and instead focus on positive things such as pursuing outside interests or perhaps returning to school for additional education.

6: What other types of jobs have you been looking for?
Answer:
The answer to this question can show the interviewer that you're both on the market and in demand. Mention jobs you've applied for or looked at that are closely related to your field, or similar to the position you're interviewing for. Don't bring up last-ditch efforts that found you applying for a part-time job completely unrelated to your field.

7: Have you ever been disciplined at work?
Answer:
Hopefully the answer here is no – but if you have been disciplined for something at work though, be absolutely sure that you can

explain it thoroughly. Detail what you learned from the situation, and reflect on how you grew after the process.

8: What is your availability like?
Answer:
Your availability should obviously be as open as possible, and any gaps in availability should be explained and accounted for. Avoid asking about vacation or personal days (as well as other benefits), and convey to the interviewer how serious you are about your work.

9: May I contact your current employer?
Answer:
If possible, it is best to allow an interviewer to contact your current employer as a reference. However, if it's important that your employer is not contacted, explain your reason tactfully, such as you just started job searching and you haven't had the opportunity yet to inform them that you are looking for other employment. Be careful of this reasoning though, as employers may wonder if you'll start shopping for something better while employed with them as well.

10: Do you have any valuable contacts you could bring to our business?
Answer:
It's great if you can bring knowledge, references, or other contacts that your new employer may be able to network with. However, be sure that you aren't offering up any of your previous employer's clients, or in any way violating contractual agreements.

11: How soon would you be available to start working?
Answer:
While you want to be sure that you're available to start as soon as possible if the company is interested in hiring you, if you still have another job, be sure to give them at least two weeks' notice.

Though your new employer may be anxious for you to start, they will want to hire a worker whom they can respect for giving adequate notice, so that they won't have to worry if you'll eventually leave them in the lurch.

12: Why would your last employer say that you left?
Answer:
The key to this question is that your employer's answer must be the same as your own answer about why you left. For instance, if you've told your employer that you left to find a position with greater opportunities for career advancement, your employer had better not say that you were let go for missing too many days of work. Honesty is key in your job application process.

13: How long have you been actively looking for a job?
Answer:
It's best if you haven't been actively looking for a job for very long, as a long period of time may make the interviewer wonder why no one else has hired you. If it has been awhile, make sure to explain why, and keep it positive. Perhaps you haven't come across many opportunities that provide you with enough of a challenge or that are adequately matched to someone of your education and experience.

14: When don't you show up to work?
Answer:
Clearly, the only time acceptable to miss work is for a real emergency or when you're truly sick – so don't start bringing up times now that you plan to miss work due to vacations or family birthdays. Alternatively, you can tell the interviewer how dedicated to your work you are, and how you always strive to be fully present and to put in the same amount of work every time you come in, even when you're feeling slightly under the weather.

15: What is the most common reason you miss work?
Answer:

If there is a reason that you will miss work routinely, this is the time to disclose it – but doing so during an interview will reflect negatively on you. Ideally, you will only miss work during cases of extreme illness or other emergencies.

16: What is your attendance record like?
Answer:
Be sure to answer this question honestly, but ideally you will have already put in the work to back up the fact that you rarely miss days or arrive late. However, if there are gaps in your attendance, explain them briefly with appropriate reasons, and make sure to emphasize your dedication to your work, and reliability.

17: Where did you hear about this position?
Answer:
This may seem like a simple question, but the answer can actually speak volumes about you. If you were referred by a friend or another employee who works for the company, this is a great chance to mention your connection (if the person is in good standing!). However, if you heard about it from somewhere like a career fair or a work placement agency, you may want to focus on how pleased you were to come across such a wonderful opportunity.

18: Tell me anything else you'd like me to know when making a hiring decision.
Answer:
This is a great opportunity for you to give a final sell of yourself to the interviewer – use this time to remind the interviewer of why you are qualified for the position, and what you can bring to the company that no one else can. Express your excitement for the opportunity to work with a company pursuing X *mission*.

19: Why would your skills be a good match with X *objective* of our company?
Answer:

If you've researched the company before the interview, answering this question should be no problem. Determine several of the company's main objectives, and explain how specific skills that you have are conducive to them. Also, think about ways that your experience and skills can translate to helping the company expand upon these objectives, and to reach further goals. If your old company had a similar objective, give a specific example of how you helped the company to meet it.

20: What do you think this job entails?
Answer:
Make sure you've researched the position well before heading into the interview. Read any and all job descriptions you can find (at best, directly from the employer's website or job posting), and make note of key duties, responsibilities, and experience required. Few things are less impressive to an interviewer than a candidate who has no idea what sort of job they're actually being interviewed for.

21: Is there anything else about the job or company you'd like to know?
Answer:
If you have learned about the company beforehand, this is a great opportunity to show that you put in the effort to study before the interview. Ask questions about the company's mission in relation to current industry trends, and engage the interviewer in interesting, relevant conversation. Additionally, clear up anything else you need to know about the specific position before leaving – so that if the interviewer calls with an offer, you'll be prepared to answer.

22: Are you the best candidate for this position?
Answer:
Yes! Offer specific details about what makes you qualified for this position, and be sure to discuss (and show) your unbridled passion and enthusiasm for the new opportunity, the job, and the

company.

23: How did you prepare for this interview?
Answer:
The key part of this question is to make sure that you have prepared! Be sure that you've researched the company, their objectives, and their services prior to the interview, and know as much about the specific position as you possibly can. It's also helpful to learn about the company's history and key players in the current organization.

24: If you were hired here, what would you do on your first day?
Answer:
While many people will answer this question in a boring fashion, going through the standard first day procedures, this question is actually a great chance for you to show the interviewer why you will make a great hire. In addition to things like going through training or orientation, emphasize how much you would enjoy meeting your supervisors and coworkers, or how you would spend a lot of the day asking questions and taking in all of your new surroundings.

25: Have you viewed our company's website?
Answer:
Clearly, you should have viewed the company's website and done some preliminary research on them before coming to the interview. If for some reason you did not, do not say that you did, as the interviewer may reveal you by asking a specific question about it. If you did look at the company's website, this is an appropriate time to bring up something you saw there that was of particular interest to you, or a value that you especially supported.

26: How does X *experience* on your resume relate to this position?
Answer:

Many applicants will have some bit of experience on their resume that does not clearly translate to the specific job in question. However, be prepared to be asked about this type of seemingly-irrelevant experience, and have a response prepared that takes into account similar skill sets or training that the two may share.

27: Why do you want this position?
Answer:
Keep this answer focused positively on aspects of this specific job that will allow you to further your skills, offer new experience, or that will be an opportunity for you to do something that you particularly enjoy. Don't tell the interviewer that you've been looking for a job for a long time, or that the pay is very appealing, or you will appear unmotivated and opportunistic.

28: How is your background relevant to this position?
Answer:
Ideally, this should be obvious from your resume. However, in instances where your experience is more loosely-related to the position, make sure that you've researched the job and company well before the interview. That way, you can intelligently relate the experience and skills that you do have, to similar skills that would be needed in the new position. Explain specifically how your skills will translate, and use words to describe your background such as "preparation" and "learning." Your prospective position should be described as an "opportunity" and a chance for "growth and development."

29: How do you feel about X *mission* of our company?
Answer:
It's important to have researched the company prior to the interview – and if you've done so, this question won't catch you off guard. The best answer is one that is simple, to the point, and shows knowledge of the mission at hand. Offer a few short statements as to why you believe in the mission's importance, and note that you would be interested in the chance to work with a

company that supports it.

30: Where do you find ideas?
Answer:
Ideas can come from all places, and an interviewer wants to see that your ideas are just as varied. Mention multiple places that you gain ideas from, or settings in which you find yourself brainstorming. Additionally, elaborate on how you record ideas or expand upon them later.

31: How do you achieve creativity in the workplace?
Answer:
It's important to show the interviewer that you're capable of being resourceful and innovative in the workplace, without stepping outside the lines of company values. Explain where ideas normally stem from for you (examples may include an exercise such as list-making or a mind map), and connect this to a particular task in your job that it would be helpful to be creative in.

32: How do you push others to create ideas?
Answer:
If you're in a supervisory position, this may be requiring employees to submit a particular number of ideas, or to complete regular idea-generating exercises, in order to work their creative muscles. However, you can also push others around you to create ideas simply by creating more of your own. Additionally, discuss with the interviewer the importance of questioning people as a way to inspire ideas and change.

33: Describe your creativity.
Answer:
Try to keep this answer within the professional realm, but if you have an impressive background in something creative outside of your employment history, don't be afraid to include it in your answer also. The best answers about creativity will relate

problem-solving skills, goal-setting, and finding innovative ways to tackle a project or make a sale in the workplace. However, passions outside of the office are great, too (so long as they don't cut into your work time or mental space).

34: How do you make decisions?
Answer:
This is a great opportunity for you to wow your interviewer with your decisiveness, confidence, and organizational skills. Make sure that you outline a process for decision-making, and that you stress the importance of weighing your options, as well as in trusting intuition. If you answer this question skillfully and with ease, your interviewer will trust in your capability as a worker.

35: What are the most difficult decisions for you to make?
Answer:
Explain your relationship to decision-making, and a general synopsis of the process you take in making choices. If there is a particular type of decision that you often struggle with, such as those that involve other people, make sure to explain why that type of decision is tough for you, and how you are currently engaged in improving your skills.

36: When making a tough decision, how do you gather information?
Answer:
If you're making a tough choice, it's best to gather information from as many sources as possible. Lead the interviewer through your process of taking information from people in different areas, starting first with advice from experts in your field, feedback from coworkers or other clients, and by looking analytically at your own past experiences.

37: Tell me about a decision you made that did not turn out well.
Answer:
Honesty and transparency are great values that your interviewer

will appreciate – outline the choice you made, why you made it, the results of your poor decision – and finally (and most importantly!) what you learned from the decision. Give the interviewer reason to trust that you wouldn't make a decision like that again in the future.

38: Are you able to make decisions quickly?
Answer:
You may be able to make decisions quickly, but be sure to communicate your skill in making sound, thorough decisions as well. Discuss the importance of making a decision quickly, and how you do so, as well as the necessity for each decision to first be well-informed.

39: What is the best way for a company to advertise?
Answer:
If you're going for a position in any career other than marketing, this question is probably intended to demonstrate your ability to think critically and to provide reflective support for your answers. As such, the particular method you choose is not so important as why you've chosen it. For example, word of mouth advertising is important because customers will inherently trust the source, and social media advertising is important as it reaches new customers quickly and cheaply.

40: Is it better to gain a new customer or to keep an old one?
Answer:
In almost every case, it is better to keep an old customer, and it's important that you are able to articulate why this is. First, new customers generally cost companies more than retaining old ones does, and new customers are more likely to switch to a different company. Additionally, keeping old customers is a great way to provide a stable backbone for the company, as well as to also gain new customers as they are likely to recommend your company to friends.

41: What is the best way to win clients from competitors?
Answer:
There are many schools of thought on the best way to win clients from competitors, and unless you know that your interviewer adheres to a specific thought or practice, it's best to keep this question general. Rather than using absolute language, focus on the benefits of one or two strategies and show a clear, critical understanding of how these ways can succeed in a practical application.

42: How do you feel about companies monitoring internet usage?
Answer:
Generally speaking, most companies will monitor some degree of internet usage over their employees – and during an interview is not the best time to rebel against this practice. Instead, focus on positive aspects such as the way it can lead to increased productivity for some employees who may be easily lost in the world of resourceful information available to them.

43: What is your first impression of our company?
Answer:
Obviously, this should be a positive answer! Pick out a couple key components of the company's message or goals that you especially identify with or that pertain to your experience, and discuss why you believe these missions are so important.

44: Tell me about your personal philosophy on business.
Answer:
Your personal philosophy on business should be well-thought out, and in line with the missions and objectives of the company. Stay focused on positive aspects such as the service it can provide, and the lessons people gain in business, and offer insight as to where your philosophy has come from.

45: What's most important in a business model: sales, customer

service, marketing, management, etc.?
Answer:
For many positions, it may be a good strategy to tailor this answer to the type of field you're working in, and to explain why that aspect of business is key. However, by explaining that each aspect is integral to the function as a whole, you can display a greater sense of business savvy to the interviewer and may stand out in his or her mind as a particularly aware candidate.

46: How do you keep up with news and emerging trends in the field?
Answer:
The interviewer wants to see that you are aware of what's currently going on in your field. It is important that your education does not stop after college, and the most successful candidates will have a list of resources they regularly turn to already in place, so that they may stay aware and engaged in developing trends.

47: Would you have a problem adhering to company policies on social media?
Answer:
Social media concerns in the workplace have become a greater issue, and many companies now outline policies for the use of social media. Interviewers will want to be assured that you won't have a problem adhering to company standards, and that you will maintain a consistent, professional image both in the office and online.

48: Tell me about one of the greatest problems facing X *industry* today.
Answer:
If you're involved in your career field, and spend time on your own studying trends and new developments, you should be able to display an awareness of both problems and potential solutions coming up in the industry. Research some of the latest news

before heading into the interview, and be prepared to discuss current events thoroughly.

49: What do you think it takes to be successful in our company?
Answer:
Research the company prior to the interview. Be aware of the company's mission and main objectives, as well as some of the biggest names in the company, and also keep in mind how they achieved success. Keep your answer focused on specific objectives you could reach in order to help the company achieve its goals.

50: What is your favorite part of working in this career field?
Answer:
This question is an opportunity to discuss some of your favorite aspects of the job, and to highlight why you are a great candidate for the particular position. Choose elements of the work you enjoy that are related to what you would do if hired for the position. Remember to remain enthusiastic and excited for the opportunities you could attain in the job.

51: What do you see happening to your career in the next 10 years?
Answer:
If you're plugged in to what's happening in your career now, and are making an effort to stay abreast of emerging trends in your field, you should be able to offer the interviewer several predictions as to where your career or field may be heading. This insight and level of awareness shows a level of dedication and interest that is important to employers.

And Finally Good Luck!

INDEX

SAS Programming Guidelines Interview Questions

Efficient SAS Programming
1: What resources are used to run a SAS program?
2: List the factors that need to be considered while assessing the technical environment.
3: Explain the functionality of the system option STIMER in the Windows environment.
4: What is the function of the option FULLSTIMER in the Windows operating environment?
5: Explain the MEMRPT option.
6: While benchmarking the programming techniques in SAS, why is it necessary to execute each programming technique in separate sessions?
7: While doing benchmark tests, when is it advisable to run the code for each programming technique several times?
8: How do you turn off the FULLSTIMER option?
9: What steps can be taken to reduce the programmer time?

Memory Usage
10: What is the sequence of action performed in the background while trying to create a data set from another data set?
11: Define page and page size.
12: What procedure is used to indicate the page size of a data set?
13: Is it possible to control the page size of an output data set?
14: What is the default value of the BUFSIZE= option?
15: Is it necessary to specify the BUFSIZE= option every time a data set is processed?
16: Explain the significance of BUFNO= option.
17: How do you set the BUFNO= option to the maximum possible number?
18: Is it necessary to specify the BUFNO= option every time a data set is processed?
19: What are the general guidelines for specifying the buffer size and buffer number in the case of small data sets?
20: How does the BUFSIZE= and BUFNO= impact the following program?

21: Explain the SASFILE statement.
22: What happens if the size of the file in the memory increases during the execution of SASFILE statement?
23: Mention the guidelines to be followed while using SASFILE statement.
24: How is free buffer allocated by the SASFILE statement?
25: Which operations are not allowed in a file opened with SASFILE statement?
26: How do you calculate the total number of bytes occupied by a data file if you know the page size?

Data Storage Space

27: What factors are considered by SAS when calculating the data storage space required for a SAS data file?
28: How do a SAS character variable store data and what is the default length of a character variable?
29: Which step can be taken to reduce the length of a character variable?
30: How does SAS store numeric values and what is the default length of a numeric variable?
31: Explain the significance of PROC COMPARE.
32: What all conditions make a data file an ideal candidate for compression?
33: Explain the compression of a data set.
34: Which option is used for accessing an observation directly in an uncompressed data set?
35: Which option is used for controlling direct access in a compressed data set?
36: Once a SAS data file is compressed, is it possible to change the setting to uncompressed?
37: Explain the significance of REUSE= option.
38: What is the main difference between a SAS data file and a SAS data view?
39: What are the sources from which SAS data view can extract the data?
40: What are the main advantages of using a data step view?
41: Explain how to create a data step view.
42: How do you check the source statement related to a DATA step view?
43: Is the code submitted to create a DATA STEP view executed?
44: What happens when a DATA STEP view is referenced in a proc step?
45: Which of these methods is more efficient when the required data is used repeatedly in a program - creating a data set or creating a data step

view?
46: How does a SAS DATA STEP VIEW handle multiple passes through the data?
47: How does the updating of observations differ in compressed data files and uncompressed data files?
48: What is the default size of view buffer?

Best Practices

49: What is the best practice to follow while sub-setting the data?
50: When is the IF-THEN/ELSE statement more used and what best practices should be followed?
51: When is the SELECT statement more suitable and what are the best practices to be followed while employing it?
52: List the best practices while calling a function.
53: Which best practice needs to be followed while creating multiple subsets of a SAS data set?
54: Which best practice needs to be followed while using the SORT procedure to sort a SAS data set?
55: What best practice needs to be followed to change the attribute of a variable?
56: While subsetting the observations is the – IF statement or Where statement more efficient?
57: How does the scope of selection of data differ in terms of IF statement and WHERE statement?
58: Which best practice needs to be followed while subsetting the data read from an external file?
59: How does the positioning of DROP= and KEEP= data set option affect the resource usage?
60: Which method helps in optimizing performance of a SAS program in regard to the storage of data?
61: Use an example to explain run group processing.
62: Explain the NOLIST option.

Sorting Strategies

63: Is there any way to avoid the use of PROC SORT by using an index?
64: What are the main disadvantages of using BY-group processing with an index?
65: Which option can be used with the by statement to create ordered or grouped reports without sorting the data?
66: The NOTSORTED option cannot be used with what two statements?

67: Is it allowed to use the NOTSORTED option along with the temporary variables – first.Variable & last.variable?
68: Explain the GROUPFORMAT option.
69: What statement other than BY statement can be used to avoid sort?
70: When is a CLASS statement preferred over a BY statement?
71: Explain the significance of SORTEDBY= dataset option.
72: What is threaded processing in SAS?
73: What are the two common constraints on the performance of a SAS application?
74: How does the SAS SPD engine support threaded I/O?
75: How can we improve the performance of CPU bound applications?
76: How can you enable threaded sorting?
77: Explain the CPUCOUNT= system option.
78: What is the range of the option CPUCOUNT=?
79: What formula is used to calculate the additional workspace required by PROC SORT?
80: Which system option is used to specify the memory available to sort procedure?
81: What happens when the space required by the workspace is greater than the value specified by SORTSIZE= system option?
82: Use an example to explain how to divide and sort a large data set using Interleaving.
83: Can PROC APPEND be used for combining the sorted sub sets while sorting large data sets?
84: While dividing and sorting large data sets, which of these uses less resources while re-creating the data sets from sorted subsets: Interleaving, appending or merging?
85: Explain the TAGSORT option.
86: How does processing time used by TAGSORT option differ from the regular sort?
87: Explain the NODUPKEY option.
88: Explain the NODUPRECS option.
89: Which alias is used in place of NUDUPRECS?
90: Explain the significance of SORTDUP= system option.
91: Explain the significance of the EQUALS sort procedure option.
92: Which option among EQUALS & NOEQUALS is the default and which saves CPU resources?
93: Illustrate the use of FIRST Processing in the DATA step to remove the duplicate observations from the dataset.
94: Explain the option SORTPGM=.

95: Explain the option SORTCUTP=.
96: What is the default value for SORTCUTP= option in the UNIX and WINDOWS operating environment?
97: Explain the option SORTCUT=.
98: Explain the option SORTNAME=.
99: Demonstrate with a program how SAS processes the observation when accessing the data sequentially using the where statement.
100: Demonstrate with a program how SAS processes the observation when accessing the data using the index along with where statement.

Samples

101: How is a systematic sample from a data set created with a known number of observations?
102: What option can be used to find the total number of observations in a data set?
103: How do you create a systematic sample from a data set whose total number of observations are unknown?
104: Explain the RANUNI function.
105: How is it possible to increase the interval of the random number generator?
106: What function is used to create a random integer?
107: What is the term used for the argument of a ranuni function?
108: Is the output produced by the ranuni function replicable?
109: What is a RANDOM SAMPLE with replacement?
110: How is a random sample with replacement created?

Using Indexes

111: Explain the purpose of using indexes.
112: Explain how to create an index at same time of data set creation.
113: How do you create an index on an already existing data set?
114: Explain how to delete an index from a data set.
115: Where is an index associated with a data set stored and under what name?
116: How is information obtained about the indexes associated with a SAS data set?
117: How is an indexed data set copied to a new location?
118: Explain the COPY PROCEDURE with an example.
119: How is an indexed data set renamed?
120: How is a variable in an indexed data set renamed?

Combining Data Vertically

121: How is a FILENAME Statement used to combine raw data files?
122: Which procedure can be used to view the structure and content of raw data files?
123: Explain the significance of the COMPRESS function.
124: How is the APPEND procedure used to concatenate two data sets?
125: What happens while using append procedure if the data set mentioned in the DATA= option has more variables than the data set mentioned in the BASE= option?
126: While using append procedure, what happens if the data set mentioned in the DATA= option has variables longer than the variables mentioned in the BASE= option?

Combining Data Horizontally

127: Use an example to illustrate the use of IF- THEN/ELSE statement for combining the data from a table with hardcoded values.
128: List the advantages and disadvantages of using IF-THEN/ELSE statement to combine the data.
129: How do you use an ARRAY statement to combine the data from a data set with a list of values?
130: State the advantages and disadvantages of using an ARRAY statement to combine data.
131: How is the format procedure used to combine the data?
132: State the advantages and disadvantages of using the format procedure to combine the data.
133: What happens when the variables in the input data sets of a MERGE statement have the same name but are different type?
134: State the advantages and disadvantages of using the match-merge procedure.
135: Illustrate the use of PROC SQL to combine the data.
136: What are the benefits and the disadvantages of using PROC SQL for combining the data sets? If any
137: What is the function of KEY= option
138: Illustrate the use of an index to combine the data sets.
139: Illustrate the use of _IORC_ variable.

Lookup Tables

140: Explain the significance of prefix= option while using PROC TRANSPOSE.

141: What option can be used with PROC TRANSPOSE to change the variable names?

Formatting Data

142: Explain the significance of the LOG statement.
143: Explain the significance of a PICTURE statement.
144: Explain the significance of DIRECTIVES.
145: Explain the functionality of FMTLIB keyword.
146: While using FMTLIB KEYWORD, is it possible to list specific format rather than entire catalog?
147: How to copy a format from one catalog to another?
148: How is a PROC CATALOG step used to list the contents of a catalog?
149: How is a format assigned to a variable in an existing data set?
150: What is the function of FMTSEARCH= system option?
151: Which libraries are searched for formats when a format is referenced?
152: Explain the significance of the FMTERR option.
153: Is it possible to create a format from a SAS data set? Explain with a program.
154: What prerequisites need to be satisfied by a SAS data set so it qualifies as a control data set?
155: Which option is used for creating a SAS data set from a format?

Tracking Changes

156: What happens when a data step is submitted to create a data set that is also mentioned in the SET statement?
157: What happens when a data step is submitted to create a data set that is also mentioned in the MODIFY statement?
158: How is a master data set modified using a transaction data set?
159: Is it necessary to sort the master data set and transaction data set before applying the MODIFY statement?
160: What happens when there are duplicate values of BY variable in the master data set or transaction data set?
161: Explain the significance of the option UPDATEMODE=.
162: How the observations located by an index modified?
163: How does an updating with INDEX differ from updating using the BY statement?
164: While using an INDEX to locate the values to be updated, how are the duplicate values handled?

165: Is it possible to use an OUTPUT statement in a DATA step that contains a modify statement?
166: What is _IORC_?
167: How can you create the INTEGRITY constraints using DATASETS PROCEDURE?
168: In what situations are integrity constraints enforced?
169: How can you view the INTEGRITY CONSTRAINTS created on a data set?
170: How is an integrity constraint removed from a data set?
171: What is an AUDIT TRAIL?
172: How is an AUDIT TRAIL initiated?
173: How do you read the contents of an AUDIT TRAIL file?
174: What are AUDIT TRAIL variables?
175: Explain the function of BEFORE_IMAGE audit setting.
176: Explain the function of ERROR_IMAGE audit setting.
177: Explain the function of DATA_IMAGE audit setting.
178: What is a user variable in an audit trail?
179: Is it possible to suspend an audit trail then resume after some time?
180: How are audit trails deleted?
181: When is a generation data set preferred over an audit trail?
182: How is generation data sets initiated?
183: Name the scenarios where a generation data set is created.
184: How are particular generations of a data set selected from a generation group?
185: Is it possible to rename the generation group once the generation data sets are created?
186: Which statement is used to delete any of the generation data sets?
187: Explain the significance of the keyword HIST.
188: What procedures are commonly used to produce a detail report?
189: Compare PROC PRINT and PROC SQL in terms of resource usage while producing a sorted subset detail report.
190: While producing a summary dataset with one or more class variables, what tools are to be used if there are a large number of distinct
191: Which summarizing tool is most efficient for a small number of distinct combinations of class variables while producing a summary data set?
192: Why is a TYPES statement used with PROC MEANS?
193: Why use NWAY option with PROC MEANS?
194: Is using WHERE= option allowed with PROC MEANS?
195: How does the size of the subset to be extracted from a data set affect

the decision to create an index?

196: Under what WHERE condition does SAS decide not to use an INDEX?

197: What is compound optimization?

198: Describe some situations in which compound optimization are not performed by SAS.

199: Explain the CENTILES option.

200: How does the number of pages in a file affect the decision to use an INDEX?

HR Questions

1: What are the three most important things you're looking for in a position?
2: How are you evaluating the companies you're looking to work with?
3: Are you comfortable working for _____ salary?
4: Why did you choose your last job?
5: How long has it been since your last job and why?
6: What other types of jobs have you been looking for?
7: Have you ever been disciplined at work?
8: What is your availability like?
9: May I contact your current employer?
10: Do you have any valuable contacts you could bring to our business?
11: How soon would you be available to start working?
12: Why would your last employer say that you left?
13: How long have you been actively looking for a job?
14: When don't you show up to work?
15: What is the most common reason you miss work?
16: What is your attendance record like?
17: Where did you hear about this position?
18: Tell me anything else you'd like me to know when making a hiring decision.
19: Why would your skills be a good match with *X objective* of our company?
20: What do you think this job entails?
21: Is there anything else about the job or company you'd like to know?
22: Are you the best candidate for this position?
23: How did you prepare for this interview?
24: If you were hired here, what would you do on your first day?
25: Have you viewed our company's website?
26: How does *X experience* on your resume relate to this position?
27: Why do you want this position?
28: How is your background relevant to this position?
29: How do you feel about *X mission* of our company?
30: Where do you find ideas?
31: How do you achieve creativity in the workplace?
32: How do you push others to create ideas?
33: Describe your creativity.
34: How do you make decisions?
35: What are the most difficult decisions for you to make?
36: When making a tough decision, how do you gather information?

37: Tell me about a decision you made that did not turn out well.
38: Are you able to make decisions quickly?
39: What is the best way for a company to advertise?
40: Is it better to gain a new customer or to keep an old one?
41: What is the best way to win clients from competitors?
42: How do you feel about companies monitoring internet usage?
43: What is your first impression of our company?
44: Tell me about your personal philosophy on business.
45: What's most important in a business model: sales, customer service, marketing, management, etc.?
46: How do you keep up with news and emerging trends in the field?
47: Would you have a problem adhering to company policies on social media?
48: Tell me about one of the greatest problems facing *X industry* today.
49: What do you think it takes to be successful in our company?
50: What is your favorite part of working in this career field?
51: What do you see happening to your career in the next 10 years?

Some of the following titles might also be handy:
1. .NET Interview Questions You'll Most Likely Be Asked
2. 200 Interview Questions You'll Most Likely Be Asked
3. Access VBA Programming Interview Questions You'll Most Likely Be Asked
4. Adobe ColdFusion Interview Questions You'll Most Likely Be Asked
5. Advanced Excel Interview Questions You'll Most Likely Be Asked
6. Advanced JAVA Interview Questions You'll Most Likely Be Asked
7. Advanced SAS Interview Questions You'll Most Likely Be Asked
8. AJAX Interview Questions You'll Most Likely Be Asked
9. Algorithms Interview Questions You'll Most Likely Be Asked
10. Android Development Interview Questions You'll Most Likely Be Asked
11. Ant & Maven Interview Questions You'll Most Likely Be Asked
12. Apache Web Server Interview Questions You'll Most Likely Be Asked
13. Artificial Intelligence Interview Questions You'll Most Likely Be Asked
14. ASP.NET Interview Questions You'll Most Likely Be Asked
15. Automated Software Testing Interview Questions You'll Most Likely Be Asked
16. Base SAS Interview Questions You'll Most Likely Be Asked
17. BEA WebLogic Server Interview Questions You'll Most Likely Be Asked
18. C & C++ Interview Questions You'll Most Likely Be Asked
19. C# Interview Questions You'll Most Likely Be Asked
20. C++ Internals Interview Questions You'll Most Likely Be Asked
21. CCNA Interview Questions You'll Most Likely Be Asked
22. Cloud Computing Interview Questions You'll Most Likely Be Asked
23. Computer Architecture Interview Questions You'll Most Likely Be Asked
24. Computer Networks Interview Questions You'll Most Likely Be Asked
25. Core JAVA Interview Questions You'll Most Likely Be Asked
26. Data Structures & Algorithms Interview Questions You'll Most Likely Be Asked
27. Data WareHousing Interview Questions You'll Most Likely Be Asked
28. EJB 3.0 Interview Questions You'll Most Likely Be Asked
29. Entity Framework Interview Questions You'll Most Likely Be Asked
30. Fedora & RHEL Interview Questions You'll Most Likely Be Asked
31. GNU Development Interview Questions You'll Most Likely Be Asked
32. Hibernate, Spring & Struts Interview Questions You'll Most Likely Be Asked
33. HTML, XHTML and CSS Interview Questions You'll Most Likely Be Asked
34. HTML5 Interview Questions You'll Most Likely Be Asked
35. IBM WebSphere Application Server Interview Questions You'll Most Likely Be Asked
36. iOS SDK Interview Questions You'll Most Likely Be Asked
37. Java / J2EE Design Patterns Interview Questions You'll Most Likely Be Asked
38. Java / J2EE Interview Questions You'll Most Likely Be Asked
39. Java Messaging Service Interview Questions You'll Most Likely Be Asked
40. JavaScript Interview Questions You'll Most Likely Be Asked
41. JavaServer Faces Interview Questions You'll Most Likely Be Asked
42. JDBC Interview Questions You'll Most Likely Be Asked
43. jQuery Interview Questions You'll Most Likely Be Asked
44. JSP-Servlet Interview Questions You'll Most Likely Be Asked
45. JUnit Interview Questions You'll Most Likely Be Asked
46. Linux Commands Interview Questions You'll Most Likely Be Asked
47. Linux Interview Questions You'll Most Likely Be Asked
48. Linux System Administrator Interview Questions You'll Most Likely Be Asked
49. Mac OS X Lion Interview Questions You'll Most Likely Be Asked
50. Mac OS X Snow Leopard Interview Questions You'll Most Likely Be Asked
51. Microsoft Access Interview Questions You'll Most Likely Be Asked

52. Microsoft Excel Interview Questions You'll Most Likely Be Asked
53. Microsoft Powerpoint Interview Questions You'll Most Likely Be Asked
54. Microsoft Word Interview Questions You'll Most Likely Be Asked
55. MySQL Interview Questions You'll Most Likely Be Asked
56. NetSuite Interview Questions You'll Most Likely Be Asked
57. Networking Interview Questions You'll Most Likely Be Asked
58. OOPS Interview Questions You'll Most Likely Be Asked
59. Operating Systems Interview Questions You'll Most Likely Be Asked
60. Oracle DBA Interview Questions You'll Most Likely Be Asked
61. Oracle E-Business Suite Interview Questions You'll Most Likely Be Asked
62. ORACLE PL/SQL Interview Questions You'll Most Likely Be Asked
63. Perl Interview Questions You'll Most Likely Be Asked
64. PHP Interview Questions You'll Most Likely Be Asked
65. PMP Interview Questions You'll Most Likely Be Asked
66. Python Interview Questions You'll Most Likely Be Asked
67. RESTful JAVA Web Services Interview Questions You'll Most Likely Be Asked
68. Ruby Interview Questions You'll Most Likely Be Asked
69. Ruby on Rails Interview Questions You'll Most Likely Be Asked
70. SAP ABAP Interview Questions You'll Most Likely Be Asked
71. Selenium Testing Tools Interview Questions You'll Most Likely Be Asked
72. Silverlight Interview Questions You'll Most Likely Be Asked
73. Software Repositories Interview Questions You'll Most Likely Be Asked
74. Software Testing Interview Questions You'll Most Likely Be Asked
75. SQL Server Interview Questions You'll Most Likely Be Asked
76. Tomcat Interview Questions You'll Most Likely Be Asked
77. UML Interview Questions You'll Most Likely Be Asked
78. Unix Interview Questions You'll Most Likely Be Asked
79. UNIX Shell Programming Interview Questions You'll Most Likely Be Asked
80. VB.NET Interview Questions You'll Most Likely Be Asked
81. XLXP, XSLT, XPATH, XFORMS & XQuery Interview Questions You'll Most Likely Be Asked
82. XML Interview Questions You'll Most Likely Be Asked

For complete list visit
www.vibrantpublishers.com

Made in the USA
Charleston, SC
07 March 2013